For Mets Fans Only

By Rich Wolfe

Published by Rich Wolfe and Lone Wolfe Press with Sams Technical Publishing, LLC, under the Life Press imprint, 9850 E.30th St., Indianapolis IN 46229.

Copies of this book can be ordered directly from the publisher at 1-800-428-7267 or at www.samswebsite.com as well as at your local bookseller or online book retailer.

The author, Rich Wolfe, can be reached at 602-738-5889.

International Standard Book Number: 0-7906-1334-4

The patch of the Mets logo used on this cover was purchased and digitally photographed for use on this cover, by the publisher

Photos provided by Rich Wolfe, *Sports Illustrated*, and Marquess Gallery, St. Louis MO.

www.marquessgallery.com
www.baseballfineart.com

Interior design from The Printed Page, Phoenix AZ.
Cover design from Mike Walsh, Phoenix AZ.

Manufactured in the USA.

> **Page Two. In 1941, the news director at a small radio station in Kalamazoo, Michigan hired Harry Caray who had been employed at a station in Joliet, Illinois. The news director's name was Paul Harvey. Yes, that <u>Paul Harvey</u>! "And now, you have the rest of the story...... ➡**

DEDICATION

To
John "Ray" Sullivan, ND '64

ACKNOWLEDGMENTS

Wonderful people helped make this book a reality, starting with Ellen Brewer in Edmond, Oklahoma and Lisa Liddy at The Printed Page in Phoenix—wonder women who have been indispensable sidekicks for many years. Ditto for Barbara Jane Bookman in Falmouth, Massachusetts. A big thanks to Sharon Tully and Carol Reddy at Lone Wolfe Press and the good guys over at Wolfegang Marketing Systems, Ltd .—But Not Very… like Jon Spoelstra, John Counsell, and Jim Murray.

How about those great people at Sam's Technical Publishing, as well as T. Roy Gaul in Bettendorf; and the Tower of Power in Ladue, Don Marquess.

Special thanks to Ira Rosen and the nice folks at Clarkson Potter and to Rhonda Sonnenberg for her many hours of research. Let's not forget Lisa Dolan in Hudson, N.Y. and the gorgeous Ellen Carr in Round Top, N.Y.

A tip of the hat to all those interviewed who missed the final cut—we just flat ran out of time and space. Three chapters were cut indiscriminately due to space limitations. It was close and we're gonna do it again next year. Thanks everyone!

PREFACE

For Mets Fans Only is part of an 81-book series to be released in the next 15 months. From Green Bay to Austin, from Notre Dame to Boston, and 76 other places, loyal followers will trumpet their neatest stories about their favorite teams. No other team's fans will have the passion or the undying craziness that characterizes all Mets fans.

For some of us, baseball recalls broken glass, broken bats and broken dreams of lingering reflections of a simpler, more innocent time.

For many of us, baseball defined our youth, still overly-impacts our adulthood, and is one of the few things, that can make you feel young and old at the same time.

And for all of us, it is—most of all—a game of memories: the transistor under the pillow, sitting outside a small store feverishly opening newly purchased baseball cards, our first uniform, learning to keep score, the dew and mosquitoes, the sounds of the radio or our first big league game. Little did many of us know that baseball would be the best math and geography teacher we would ever have…and none of us knew the vibrant green of the field during our first major league game would be the lushest green, the greenest green, and the most memorable green that we would ever see in our entire lifetime.

Since the age of ten, I've been a serious collector of sports books. During that time—for the sake of argument, let's call it 30 years—my favorite book style is the eavesdropping type where the subject talks in his or her own words—without the "then he said" or "the air was so thick you could cut it with a butter knife" waste of verbiage that makes it so hard to get to the meat of the matter. Books such as Lawrence Ritter's *Glory of*

Their Times and Donald Honig's *Baseball When the Grass Was Real*. Thus, I adopted that style when I started compiling oral histories of the Mike Ditkas and Harry Carays of the world. I'm a sports fan first and foremost—I don't even pretend to be an author. Literally, I can't type and I've never turned on a computer. I'm just an old guy who loves sports books and was lucky enough to develop a format that most baseball fans really enjoy. This book is designed solely for other sports fans. I really don't care what the publisher, editors, or critics think. I'm only interested in Mets fans having an enjoyable read and getting their money's worth. Sometimes a person being interviewed will drift off the subject but if the feeling is that baseball fans would enjoy the digression, it stays in the book.

In an effort to get more material into the book, the editor decided to merge some paragraphs and omit some of the punctuation, which will allow for the reader to receive an additional 20,000 words, the equivalent of 50 pages. More bang for your buck… more fodder for English teachers…fewer dead trees.

As stated on the dust jacket, there have been over a hundred books written about the Mets but not a single one about Mets fans—until now. From one baseball fan to another, I sincerely wish you enjoy this unique format.

Hopefully, the stories you are about to read will bring back wonderful memories of your youth and growing allegiance to the Mets. Wouldn't it be nice to have a do-over? It just seems that sometimes, as you get older, the things that you want most are the things that you once had.

Go now.

Rich Wolfe
Celebration, Florida

CHAT ROOMS

Chapter 1

Growin' Up With the Mets

There's No Expiration Date on Dreams

DOG DAY AFTERNOON

Steve Cunetta

Steve Cunetta grew up in East Flatbush. Brooklyn is a long way from Seattle where Cunetta is a barrister.

I came up in Little League in 1967, the same year Tom Seaver joined the Mets. Of course, I wanted to be a baseball player when I grew up. I would have these incredible fantasies of myself being sort of a young player in my first year, pinch-hitting for an aging Tom Seaver and winning the game with a big hit—actually having an opportunity to pinch-hit in the late innings for this guy who was a god to me.

When the Mets so unceremoniously dumped Seaver, that was a difficult time for me. At his press conference, he commented that the Mets fans had been just great to him, and he started crying, and had his head down with his hand covering his eyes. You could hear him mutter to himself, "Come on George." It must have been one of the reporters who said, "Are you going to miss them, Tom?" He just nodded his head "Yes." I remember getting so emotional from that. It was the wrong way for him to leave the city, leave the Mets. It was just wrong....

When I was a kid I was on my own a lot. I spent the better part of my childhood watching and listening to Mets games. I would get the Mets game on the radio in my bedroom. Like a lot of fans, I was a creature of ritual. I knew a particular batter would do well if I could bounce my Spaldeen off the wall in my room and catch it in my hands a certain number of times between pitches. If I got it done, something good was going to happen. If I blew it—if I dropped it—something bad was going to happen.

I watched every Mets game broadcast on TV. I used to take a loaf of white Wonder Bread, and sit in front of the TV. By the time the game was over, half the loaf of bread would be gone. I'd have my baseball bat with me. On the broadcasts, the camera would be positioned behind the catcher. So, the camera was behind home plate and you could see the pitches come in. Our living room was just big enough where, if I didn't swing my bat full force, there was enough room to bring it around. I would mimic all the players' actions. When they took their phantom swings or practice swings, I would do the same in front of the television set. Then, I would test my ability to figure out whether the actual pitch was a strike or a ball by swinging the bat as the pitch came in. You have to imagine me, a little kid in my living room, putting the bread down, standing up with the bat and taking some swings.

In the late sixties, early seventies, the Mets had a left-handed first baseman named Mike Jorgensen. He had a way of doing phantom swings where he sort of gently dropped his bat really low and swung back and forth. When I was about ten, I was doing my phantom Mike Jorgensen swings—really gently, but still—a bat's a lethal weapon—when my dog, Daisy, decided to walk into the path of the bat. She was knocked out cold, and I was sure I had killed her.

I ran to the window and screamed out for my brother who was outside. "Michael, I killed Daisy." My parents had gone to the movies, and my grandparents, who were ostensibly watching me, lived in the apartment below. My older brother came running in, then my grandfather came in. Daisy was still out cold. She had her own little chair and they lifted her and put her in it. My grandmother got some ice for her head. I was beside myself. It was awful.

When I think back on this, the funny thing was that my grandfather, an infinitely practical man, said, in an attempt to make me feel better as I was bawling, "It's okay, Steva, the doga, she gonna be okay." He paused for a few seconds. He'd gotten close to making me feel better, when he said, "And ifa she die, I get you another one." I just burst into tears again.

The dog eventually came to, and I tell you she had a lot of respect for me after that. She never came anywhere near me when the Mets were on television.

Steinbrenner's the Boss. Boss spelled backwards is Double S.O.B.

WHEN THE METS FUTURE WAS HISTORY

Peter Kreutzer

A native of Mineola, Long Island, Peter Kreutzer, 50, is a writer and a Rotisserie League tycoon

The Yankees had been my team when I was four, five, and six, but my grandfather was a Dodgers fan, and my father was a rabid **GIANTS** fan who talked a lot about going to the Polo Grounds. So there was a built-up National League fandom among my relatives when the Mets came into existence in 1962, when I was six. We would either go visit my grandfather every Sunday, or he would come visit our family. When he came to our house, my grandfather would sit out in his car and listen to the ball game on the radio.

I inherited from my grandfather the notebooks that had imaginary box scores for every game of the season of the regular Giants' schedule that he had played in his bedroom when he was a boy. He had made up this game, where he would roll one die, and that would determine whether a ball, or a strike, or a hit were struck. Then if it were struck, he would either roll two dice or three dice. There were calculated odds so players on average hit about what average players hit.

The game had this great flaw by which all the players played off the same numbers. They had no personalities. Later, I modified my grandfather's game so the players' numbers were based on

> In 1916, the **GIANTS** had a 26-game winning streak. When they started the streak they were in fourth place and when they finally lost, they were still in fourth place.

their own stats and they were more specific to an individual player's skills....

The Mets were this incredible thing—when they started playing they were so inept. The Yankees went from being interesting and good in the 1960s to being just...well, the bottom fell out. They fired Yogi. The Mets didn't get any better, but they were the milder team. They were more like a hometown team. I remember the players would ride the train and visit all the stations. They came to my town, Smithtown, and Ed Kranepool and Ron Swoboda would sit at the train station and sign autographs and talk to the kids who showed up. Players then felt it was just part of their job. Players now don't do it but the fact of the matter is half the kids today would probably be working for autograph collectors who would send the same kid up over and over with baseballs.

I had an Ed Kranepool autograph that was written just on a chip of corrugated cardboard that I must have picked up off the ground. I don't know why he even signed it, or why I even wanted it. I became obsessed with baseball, not in any extraordinary way, but the way boys are. I'd wake up in the morning and think about the game from the night before. I collected baseball cards. I would go steal baseball cards after church from the stationery store. My parents were trustees or something like that so they had to stick around at church. There's a lot of down-time when your parents are active in the church. My obsession became going to games every year, and I'd read the programs and get the yearbook and put the pictures in my room and study everybody's stats and do all those things. I memorized everything, and I read everything. I knew everybody's story. I don't anymore, but I did. I would make up mock lineups, and I worked really hard to try and make the team better.

When I was very young, we lived next door to a salesman for the Topps company, and he would bring home the rolls of fresh cards. All my baseball cards were crooked because I wasn't very good with scissors. We played games with the cards but I never understood trading them.

Ed Kranepool was a great player. I remember Tim Harkness. He had a little bit of skill, but I think one day he might have gone five for five. It was like the greatest day in the team's history up to that point that a Met got five hits.

Seaver had been drafted by the **BRAVES**, but because of a technical irregularity, he was thrown back. A special draft was held and a few teams chose to go after him and the Mets won that special draft, so it was like a second chance.

There was something symbolic when he turned out to be good. He won sixteen games that rookie year for a terrible, terrible team. He had come up in 1967 and when he signed it must have been a year or two before that. He had pitched at the **UNIVERSITY OF SOUTHERN CALIFORNIA** and was drafted in the June draft. I don't remember what the irregularity was, but the Braves screwed up. His first year with the Mets was in 1967. He only pitched a year in the minors.

Seaver became the major talk among Mets fans. Before that, the Mets' stars were like Frank Thomas, who hit thirty-four home runs. Also there was really a lot of talk about how silly the team was—Marv Throneberry and people like that who were jokes.

> **Who is the only major league manager to later become** *Time* **magazine's Man of the Year? BRAVES owner, Ted Turner managed Atlanta for one game in 1977 before being removed by Commissioner Bowie Kuhn... Kuhn's high school basketball coach was Red Auerbach.**

> **O. J. Simpson, the great <u>USC</u> running back, and Ernie Banks are cousins. Their grandfathers were twin brothers.**

So Kranepool and Seaver were young players who were the foundation, and going into 1969 nobody knew how good Koosman and **MCANDREW** and those guys would be. The assumption was that they would go on and be terrible forever—even among Met fans. I was somebody who hoped against hope that in 1968 they would finish in ninth place instead of tenth place, that they would no longer be the worst team in the National League. I don't think anybody dreamed that they would turn around so quickly.

When the Mets and the Yankees were both pretty bad, the Mets were more interesting. The Mets logo was a cherubic baby in diapers so there was this whole feeling of birth and growing. There hadn't been expansion teams before that really, so it felt like it was going to take a long time before they could catch up with everybody else.…

Banner Day was a huge promotion. It became synonymous with the Mets and what the Mets were all about. It was usually held in July on a Sunday when they would play a doubleheader. Between games, all the fans that brought banners would be allowed on the field. Then they would parade around and prizes would be given for the best banners. It was always a sellout, and if there were any reason why we didn't go it was because it was sold out. Whenever we went, we would make a banner that would say something—we tried to be more playful than "Let's Go Mets."…

It wasn't unusual for me to do the lineups for the next day's game. At night under the covers, with a flashlight, I would write

> **In the first 45 years of Mets history, no Met pitcher threw a no-hitter…but Jim MCANDREW of Lost Nation, Iowa retired 27 Montreal batters without a hit in one game for the Mets. After Mack Jones tripled with two out in the second inning, no Expo hit safely until Jones tripled again off McAndrew with two outs in the eleventh.**

them down. I sent the Mets letters at times saying it would be so much better if they would do this or do that. I don't remember getting mad at them then, but I must have since I was motivated by their not doing things the most effective way. It's like sports talk radio—thinking I knew better than what they were doing.

As I grew older and more independent, my fandom became muted. By the time I was fifteen, I was no longer turning to the sports section first, but to the movie section and movie reviews. Through high school I was still a fan and would follow the games and watch the games on TV. Then, I began to get more interested in girls and more social things, and baseball wasn't a big part of that. There was kind of dark period there in the 1970s when I didn't follow baseball very much at all. I became more of a hippie. I was in marches and worked with the Vietnam Veterans Against the War. I attended Pitzer College in Claremont, California for two years and wound up one of those summers in Boston and didn't go to one baseball game; so I guess that means something....

At one point, I stopped being a fan of teams. I grew to really dislike ownership, and I grew to really dislike the idea that there was a false idea of teams. I spent a lot of time as a kid trying to come up with ways that teams could really represent their geography. If you were a New York team, you only had New York players. That sort of integrity really interests me. What I liked was that the team would mean something. I felt the same way about the Olympics then. I thought they meant something because everybody was from one country. I've grown quite a bit away from that viewpoint in the last twenty years.

Labor troubles came to baseball, and I remember sitting in Shea Stadium in 1981 when the fifty-day strike was starting. They were turning out the lights, and we continued to sit in our seats at Shea Stadium until the ushers came—actually it was the police who came down and kicked us out. The ushers had gone home. It felt like the end of the world at that point, that they would never play baseball again. They didn't for fifty days.

I lived in Brooklyn, and during those fifty days, I'd go up to Prospect Park and I'd watch the kids play Little League. I grew not to care all that much whether it was the Mets or the Yankees or Royals or whoever. Playing fantasy baseball does this, too. It just made the teams much less important than the players and what they do, how the players in any given situation work together.

What's the definition
of gross sports
ignorance?

144 Yankee Fans

COLD PIZZA

Vincent Rotolo

The son of a Yankee fan, Vincent Rotolo teaches 600 kids youth baseball at Pier 40 on the West Side. Turnabout is fair play, as his son is a Yankee fan.

During the 1986 World Series, when I was about thirteen, I was working as a waiter at a local pizza place on Bleeker Street in the Village. On a nearby corner, there was a Mexican restaurant and bar called The Cab Company. The restaurant had a big-screen TV, so I would leave the pizza parlor while my customers were waiting for their food and run up the street to the restaurant and look through the window to see what was going on in the games. It was October, and it was cold outside. I'm wearing a little short-sleeved T-shirt peeking through the window trying to watch Game 7, with my customers' pizzas sitting there getting cold. That was the moment when I saw the parachutist.

I was standing on a garbage can because I was too short to see. I got so excited to see the parachutist coming down that I forgot where I was and started cheering and fell off the garbage can. It was embarrassing with all the people around, but I didn't care. When I went back to work, my boss told me, "Listen, I'm sorry, but you can't work here anymore because all your pizzas are here getting cold and your customers are waiting and you're up the street watching the game." He was a good family friend, but he had to let me go. I never told my parents the truth why I was fired. I told them I needed to get better grades in school, and the job was taking too much time. But I really got fired because I was watching the game.

When I was about eight years old, I began to hang out with one of my neighbors, Raymond Dolan, who must have been in his nineties and was the oldest guy on my street. I had never met either one of my grandfathers, and Mr. Dolan was my version of granddad. He was a huge Mets fan. He would turn the color off on his little TV, and we would watch in black and white because he was so used to that. We'd be sitting there talking about old baseball days and watching the Mets. He made a huge impression on me. He passed away when I was about ten, but as a kid, he was my buddy, my friend. Most of the old-time guys were Yankee fans, because the Mets were a new team, but he was the only old-time guy around that really loved the Mets. He was just a National League fan and was really upset that the Dodgers had left. He was an old Giants fan, too, and was upset when they left.

Mr. Dolan really appreciated infield play. He had been a short-stop when he played. He was really, really old, and he was very laid back, but any time they turned a double play, or any spectacular play was made by the shortstop or any of the infielders, he would be really animated. He was a big fan of Rafael Santana and some of the really good shortstops. He was like a kid again. It was the last few years of his life, and I think baseball was all he had. Every weekend morning, I would go check in with him, and he would give me a dollar or two to go buy a **LOTTERY** ticket. I'm sure he was trying to win to leave something to his family—kind of at the end of your life and you want to leave something behind....

Growing up, Wally Backman and Lenny Dykstra were my favorite players. I really loved Roger McDowell when he was a Met.

Former Dallas Cowboy Thomas "Hollywood" Henderson won 28-million dollars in 2000 in the Texas LOTTERY... former Red Sox pitcher, Maury McDermott won millions in the Arizona Lottery the same year.

He made me laugh a lot. He was a really funny guy, a practical joker type. He was always messing around with his teammates in the bullpen, keeping guys loose, wearing a rally cap and playing jokes on other guys. I met **RON DARLING** once when I was a kid. He was really nice to me. Sometimes you meet stars in person and they disappoint you. I met Patrick Ewing. I was a big fan of his, and I was very disappointed. He wouldn't sign my autograph, and he was mean. But Ron Darling made me feel pretty good. I said to him, "Hey, I'm a fan. Can you sign this?" And he did. I still have the autograph.

RON DARLING won the pitcher's Gold Glove in 1989. Greg Maddux won the next 13.

Callin' Steinbrenner "Georgie" is like callin' Attila the Hun "Tilly"

UNCLE BOB DIDN'T KNOW ANYTHING ABOUT HORSES. HE KNEW THEY HAVE FOUR LEGS, GIVE MILK, THAT'S ABOUT IT

Leo Egan

Leo Egan was raised on Long Island and is entering his fifth decade as a Mets fan.

When I was seven years old, I went to a Mets game one July afternoon, and it was real hot. It was taking a while to get out of the Shea parking lot, and I barfed in the backseat of the car. I remember my father saying, "I am never, ever taking you to another baseball game again in your life." Of course, it wasn't true, but at the time I felt bad enough for throwing up in the back of the car. I didn't want to think that was the last time I was ever going to a ball game.

My best friend, Jamie, lived across the street. His grandmother, who at the time was in her mid-eighties, was a real character. She was just a real, real character. She was Scottish and used to caddy and golf when she was a little girl over in **SCOTLAND**. She was a great golfer, and that was at a time when girls were not allowed on the golf course.

In 1971, I was over at Jamie's house, hanging out and watching the Mets play the Dodgers on TV. His grandmother was sitting on the couch. She said, "Jamie, Jamie, who's that pitching? Is that Zack Wheat?" We didn't know who Zack Wheat was at the

> While playing golf in 1567, Mary, Queen of <u>SCOTS</u>, was informed that her husband, Lord Darnley, had been murdered. She finished the round.

time. We looked at each other like, "Who the heck is Zack Wheat?" We brushed it off. Well, I had a baseball encyclopedia and I went and looked up Zack Wheat. He retired in 1927 and he wasn't even a pitcher! We just thought it was the funniest thing that here she was watching the Mets and thought Zack Wheat was pitching....

My father's best friend collected baseball cards. The reason he collected the cards was because when he played Strat-O-Matic baseball, he would attach the real card to the player's game card so that when he rolled the dice and said, "Okay, six, Onix Concepcion," he would have Onix's card taped to the back of the Strato-O-Matic card to enhance the experience. To make them fit the Strat-O-Matic cards, he used to cut down his baseball cards. The killer of it is that the cards would be worth thousands and thousands of dollars today had he not cut them up.

Uncle Bob, as we called him, wouldn't go to the bubblegum store to get baseball cards, but instead would order the whole set by mail from **TOPPS** and get, literally, a whole shoe box full of them. I remember it was such a big thrill going to his house. I used to have maybe a hundred and fifty cards out of six hundred and fifty, but he had them all.

Flipping baseball cards is a big part of my memory. I sat on the corner and flipped cards. Each baseball team had a certain graphic that would be around the border of the card. If it was solids, you'd flip until you matched the player's card underneath, and then you would take the pot. Let's say a guy put down a blue. Say the border of the Yankees was a dark blue. Let's say the border of the Detroit Tigers was a dark blue. If a kid put down a Detroit Tiger card, and the next card you put down was a Yankee, and it was the same blue, solid, like dark blue, you got

> **In the very first set of <u>TOPPS</u> baseball cards, the first card (#1) was Andy Pafko.**

the pot. Let's say, for example, the border around a **KANSAS CITY ROYALS** card was a pale blue. If you were playing shades, you took the pot because it was blue. Solids had to be much more precise. So the pot went back and forth a lot more with shades than with solids. Flipping is how a lot of kids acquired their baseball card collections.

Uncle Bob was an accountant by trade, but he loved the **HORSES**. He always thought he had a system for betting, but he was a very quirky guy. I remember one time being out at his mother's house, and his wife Peggy had made him a drink. Well, the ice cubes in his drink had to be either vertical or horizontal, I can't remember which. She had put them the opposite way. He blew a gasket. I was about ten years old at the time, and I remember thinking this was really wacky—the direction your ice cubes are laying makes a real difference!

So, this was the guy who cut up the baseball cards so they fit exactly. They couldn't be off. It could have been that the earlier baseball cards were smaller, and to make the later cards match the earlier cards, he had to cut them down. I don't know. He was a Dodger fan first and then became a big Mets fan. Every time we went to see Uncle Bob, we talked baseball.

> In the 1979 baseball draft, the **KANSAS CITY ROYALS** selected Dan Marino in the fourth round and John Elway in the 18th round. That same year the Royals hired Rush Limbaugh for their group sales department. Limbaugh left in 1984 for a radio opportunity in California.

> In what sport was Chris Evert the leading money winner in 1974? The answer: **HORSE** racing. The owner, Carl Rosen, named his horses after tennis players. The horse named Chris Evert won $551,063 with five wins in eight starts.

I don't remember actually going to a Mets Banner Day, but I remember one time watching on TV two guys carrying a big banner that said, "What the heck happened to Schneck?" Dave Schneck was a prospect, and when the Mets brought him up, he was a bomb. Why I remember that banner, I have no idea. I thought it was the most hilarious banner I'd ever seen in my life.

I could have been a Yankee fan but the dog beat me over the fence

Yankee fans are proof that Hell is full and the dead are walking the Earth

SEATTLE:
NICE WEATHER IF YOU'RE A CROP

Kevin Martinez

Kevin Martinez, 38, grew up in Edison, New Jersey, and is now a Senior Vice President of the Seattle Mariners.

W e lived on Kester Drive in Edison and we referred to ourselves as the "Kester Kids." Every family on the block seemed to be comprised of boys about the same age. At first, we played on lawns, but parents became very upset that we were tearing up their lawns, so we migrated to the driveways, using the garage doors as backstop and strike zone. There would be about four games being played on the street at the same time. We gave different baseball park names to everybody's house. You would hear everybody doing Bob Murphy, everybody talking like Bob Murphy! "*Today the New York Mets A will take on the New York Mets B team.*" It was silly, but it was wonderful.

My brothers, Kyle and Keith, who were six and eight years older than me, would walk by and act like, "What is wrong with these guys?" But, we talked like Bob Murphy so much that they even got into the spirit. To this day, when Kyle leaves a voice mail for me at work or home, he leaves it in Bob Murphy's voice. Kyle still has the little square of tarp he cut with a pocketknife when he ran on the field at the winning game of the 1973 National League Championship Series.

My friend, Vin and I, would play Wiffle Ball just about every day after school. We were so big into the Mets that we both wanted to "BE" the Mets. What a dilemma it was, deciding who would be the Mets on any given day. We were sure we were two of the biggest Met fans in all of Jersey. We had a draft every year at the beginning of the baseball season. We drafted from the Mets current forty-man roster, and we formed our own teams. It was so much fun.

In 1980, when I was fourteen, the Mets had a Photo Day and invited the fans out onto the warning track. We were all busily taking photos of players. The problem was that the players were in the outfield at their positions, walking around. You couldn't really get any close-ups. Some of the guys came over and posed with a fan or two, but it probably wasn't going along as well as the fans wanted.

Suddenly, Frank Taveras, in shallow left field, motioned to us to come out onto the field. He was sitting out there goofing around. He had his hat flipped up forward in the front, and this little group of fans said, "He wants us to come out there. We can't go out there." Again, Taveras motioned, and you know New York fans, you tell us twice and we're going.

As the fans ran out to Frank, there was a domino effect around the warning track, and all the fans began running onto the field. Back in 1980, there weren't a ton of people in the ball park. We were on the field taking pictures, and we were hugging Frank, and high-fiving Frank, and he was having the time of his life. My good friend and I got the great idea to run out to the wall and pose like Cleon Jones and Tommie Agee. We went up to a couple of different pennants and tried to make a catch against each one. The stadium looked so huge from out there. Being on the field at Shea was a special moment I'll never forget.

THEY PUT THE FUN BACK IN FUNERAL

Charlie Ilardi

Charlie Ilardi is a video engineer and a second-generation Mets fan. Ilardi is a native of Oakland, New Jersey, and a huge Tom Seaver backer.

Mel Rojas, who came from the Chicago Cubs, was the worst pitcher the Mets ever had. My brother-in-law from Chicago warned me about him. He was the kind of pitcher who could have great stuff in the bullpen and then come out to the mound and throw a gopher ball right down the middle of the plate. Nineteen-ninety-eight was the year the Mets slogan was: "Show up at Shea." My friends and I could not believe that the Mets paid a public relations person to come up with that slogan. Why didn't they have: "Drive in and park in the parking lot and come in the gate at Shea."

Well, I got a call one day at work that the father of a close high school friend had died suddenly, and the wake was going to be that night. My friend had moved to Albany with his family so I hadn't seen him in quite some time.

It was an Irish wake, so there we were, his dad was laid out in the front, and there was crying during one half and drinking during the other half. I went up to my friend, but I was kind of at a loss for words. I said, "What happened?" My friend said, "Well, Friday night he was up late in front of the TV watching a baseball game, and the next morning he was gone."

In an effort to lighten the mood, I said, "Well, was it a Mets game?" Have you ever heard the expression, "Someone gets a twinkle in their eye?" My friend got a twinkle in his eye. His whole demeanor changed. He said, "Well, you know, yes, it was a Mets game. It was the game that Mel Rojas threw a one-two-three inning, and we think the strain was just too much for him."

I could not believe my friend, at his own father's funeral, could come up with a line like that. There's almost no reaction you could have in the middle of the funeral parlor, but I went down to my knees. I couldn't believe it. I held in my laugh and just sank to my knees. My father could only hope that I could do that at his funeral, come up with a line like that. To me, that's the best Mets story ever…

We used to get white T-shirts, and make Mets jerseys out of them with a laundry pencil. Harry's favorite player was Johnny Lewis, whose number was twenty-four, and played right field for the 1965 Mets. Harry would always tell me who to be so I was probably somebody he didn't like. My father was designated "Jack Fisher" because Fisher was a not-very-good rotund pitcher. My father was also rotund and worked for a company called Fisher. For that reason, my father seemed to like Jack Fisher. My brother and I didn't. I think Jack Fisher was eight and twenty-two in 1966.

We loved to watch Lindsey Nelson. We didn't have color TV, but even on black and white you could tell how outlandish the colors of his jackets were. When the Mets clinched the National League East in 1969, Lindsey Nelson was in the clubhouse interviewing players. He and Ralph Kiner were both there, but Kiner left to do *Kiner's Korner*. The Mets had a player named Jim Bibby, who, I don't think ever played with the parent club, and was the brother of Henry Bibby, the basketball player. He was very tall. I remember Lindsey Nelson saying "Here's Jim Bibby," and when Jim Bibby stood up on the podium, he towered over Lindsey, and Lindsey added, "Big Jim Bibby."

The *Kiner's Korner* the day after that game had about six or seven guests whereas usually the most they would have would be two or three. Tug McGraw read the HFC ad, which was very hard. I remember he stopped and called over to somebody, "Would you please hold the cue card higher?"

Kiner's Korner was just the greatest show. First, because he had this unusual way of speaking, where he was usually looking down at his cards. You got the feeling that if he looked up from the card, he would get lost. Kiner really knew his baseball history—it was only when he was calling a game that he got into trouble. In those days, there were only three announcers who covered TV and radio. Sometimes Kiner would be by himself on the radio. That was an experience. You'd hear something like, "This ball's hit deep to left, it's going, going and Harrelson backs up and makes the catch behind the second base bag!" He would often misjudge where the ball was going to be.

I particularly liked when the Mets put their twenty-five year history tape together. They snuck in a terrific Kinerism in the end credits, which most people missed. They showed a montage, and there was a home run by Donn Clendenon from 1969. Kiner said, "And this ball's hit deep to left field, way back," but the ball was plainly going toward the large scoreboard-shaped object that's in right field.

Initially, my brother and I didn't like Bob Murphy because our father looked a little like him, in that they were both kind of round. My brother and I were very angry with our father for many years. I was born in Oakland, New Jersey, and bucking the trend of the sixties, our family moved from suburbia to the inner city South Bronx when I was four years old. My brother and I resented our father for taking us from New Jersey to New York, even though we found out later he was not responsible for it and, in fact, had been very much against it. He was simply doing my mother's bidding.

Bob Murphy became our favorite announcer in later years, but our dislike of him in those early years came to a climax in 1969 when Seaver threw his near-perfect game against the Chicago Cubs. As a result of the regular rotation of the television announcers, Bob Murphy was going to be the play-by-play man for the ninth inning. My brother and I were very upset by that. We didn't like him, and were sure he was going to jinx it—something was going to go wrong. And when Jimmy Qualls, in fact, did get the base hit, that only confirmed our suspicions. It just shows you how emotional baseball can get.

In the 1980s, I loved to regale my friends with how Bob Murphy would introduce a Channel 9 broadcast. He would say, "I'm **BOB MURPHY**, with Lindsey Nelson and Ralph Kiner, and we're all set with our color telecast of today's game between the New York Mets and the Cincinnati Reds. It's a beau-u-u-tiful day for a ball game, and the Mets players are taking the field. Let's introduce them." Then I—imitating him—would introduce the players always ending with "Wa—y—ne Garrett around at third"—you had to stretch that out as long as you could. It always ended with, "and pitching for the Mets, Tom Seaver. The young right-hander from Fresno, California is having a mar-r-r-velous year." His drawl was just terrific. Bob Murphy gave a talk in the late 1980s and I finally got to meet him, which was great. He's just a great guy.

It's funny, Kiner, who's had some health troubles of late, actually became even more honest with his remarks as the years went on. He talked about how much he hated M. Donald Grant, for instance. It was great. He would tell a story and he would say who the good guy and the bad guy was, and he wouldn't pull punches, which was very interesting.

> **BOB MURPHY'S** brother had a Major League stadium named for him, Jack Murphy Stadium in San Diego. Jack Murphy was an influential San Diego sports editor who lobbied vigorously for Major League Baseball to expand to San Diego in the '60s.

CHICO ESQUELA BASEBALL CARDS ARE SELLIN' LIKE HOTCAKES... $2 A STACK

Darren DeVivo

Darren DeVivo is from the Morris Park area of the Bronx and went to high school in New Rochelle, New York.

I went to a very small Catholic high school, Salesian High School. Because it was a small school, you had a more intimate relationship with everyone—whether you wanted it or not. We were pretty close to the priests who were regular guys and would be out on the court shooting basketball after class. When it came to baseball, though, it seemed as though most were Yankee fans.

One priest who I had as a teacher early in high school, Brother Vince Bové, was the Yankees' chaplain at the time. He even wrote a book about the Yankees, and almost everyone in class had bought a copy of it, but I hadn't. It came right down to the end of the year, and Brother Vince realized that I hadn't bought his book. I think his feelings were a little hurt. But my attitude was: "It's a Yankee book." Finally, I broke down and bought one, and he signed it to me, "It's been a great year, and have a good summer." I don't have the book anymore, but it was a nice memory for me because he was a nice priest, and I missed him when he didn't come back the following September. I remember that he had interviewed Yankee players like Yogi Berra, and his book wasn't so much them talking about their team, but had to do more with their spiritual side.

In fifth grade I met a kid, Lou Mazza, who became one of my best friends. We were both Mets fans through the lean years. We went to high school together for only one year, and then he transferred out. We totally lost touch with one another, even though we lived in the same vicinity. We had taken different paths. He had started to hang out with, and be one of the "bad kids."

One day in the big 1986 season, I was in the men's bathroom at Shea Stadium. I came out and who was there, but my old friend, Lou. We went nuts. Memories came flying back. It was great, but once I left him, I was more surprised at the coincidence than anything. I guess, in my mind, he was still somebody I attached bad memories to.

A year later, in the upper deck, same vicinity, who do I bump into again, but Lou. The Mets had a "Paul McCartney Flaming Pie Night" at Shea Stadium. They played some Beatles and some solo McCartney songs between innings. It was a goofy tie-in—they didn't give anything away—but I made sure I was at the stadium for this strange link between my two loves. After that, Lou and I had a couple more chance meetings, and that led to our getting things patched up. We had grown up together, there was a lot of water under the bridge, and now we're tighter than we ever were. We've gone to many Mets games together the past several years.

Lou and I and a bunch of my other old Mets friends will, out of the blue, fire the most obscure Mets names at each other. Names like Kevin Kobel, that make us say, "You've got to be kidding me." The other day I sent a friend an e-mail and instead of my name I signed it, "John Strohmayer." My friend came back, "Who the hell is John Strohmayer?" Or, Ike Hampton, who caught about five games with the '74 Mets. Even though the Yanks were coming back into superiority by 1976 and '77, there were die-hard, cellar-dwelling Mets fans like us who remember guys like Randy Tate. He was an awful pitcher, who nearly pitched a no-hitter, yet lost it to the Montreal Expos. Those things you remember. So I'll write, "Dear Lou, We've got to meet tomorrow for dinner at ten. (signed) Randy Tate." Silly things like that.

LINDSEY NELSON DRESSED LIKE A FLOOD VICTIM

Kathy Filak

Kathy Filak, 41, is from Jersey City and has scores to settle with her brothers.

We lived on a dead-end street in Jersey City, and I remember people running up and down the street in 1969 screaming because the Mets had won the World Series. I always remembered one man running in particular, a man named **JESUS**, but I probably just remember him for his name.

My birthday is July 1, same day as Mets sportscaster Lindsey Nelson's. I took such ribbing because of his jackets, and the fact that I was born on his birthday. My brothers abused me endlessly over that. They would say, "Oh God, Lindsey Nelson and Kathy. You're gonna dress like him." The sports jacket I remember best was made of color fabric printed with the **SUNDAY COMICS**. He had the tackiest clothes.

I have two brothers who were also Mets fans. Ron is three years younger and Doug is two years older. I think they encouraged me to be a Mets fan because they were Mets fans. We devised a

> **Graffiti seen in a Nebraska truck stop, 1973:**
> (Written on wall)   *The answer is JESUS.*
> (Written below)   *What is the question?*
> (Written below)   *The question is: What is the name of Matty Alou's brother?*

> Over 1,700 of the Peanuts **COMIC** strips had a baseball theme.

game that Doug and I used to play. He would be Tom Seaver, and I would be Nancy Seaver because I just idolized her. She was this blond woman, young, pretty. I really looked up to her. I remember her being someone a little girl would definitely want to look like. And then the 'hero baseball player' husband-type thing. Doug, as Tom, would always say that he was pitching, and I, as Nancy, had a baby, although I don't know if they did actually at that time, but they probably did because we tried to model it pretty closely to reality.

I would take out a folding chair, and I would sit in front of the television, and I would watch the Mets because "Tom" was pitching. I would talk to myself and talk to the imaginary person next to me, and say, "Oh look, he got another strike." All this while, Doug would be outside playing. That was his way of getting me not to be out there bothering him. I really tried to match the games, and depending on the weather, I would sometimes put a sweater on. I don't know when or how Doug came up with that, but he would say, "Yeah, you have to watch the game. You have to be in the stands." I would just say, "Okay." I was probably seven or eight, and I think it only lasted one summer into the fall, and then by the next summer I was onto him. But that didn't stop me from watching the Mets.

Tug McGraw—I loved that, "You Gotta Believe." And the way he would always tap his mitt close to his hip. I heard that was his signal to his wife to say, "I Love You." I thought it was real sweet.

My all-time favorite player was Rusty Staub. The kid living next door had a Rusty Staub trading card. He was just an obnoxious little kid and I wanted that card badly. He bartered with me until I paid him five dollars for the card. To this day, I really like Rusty. He did nice things for people. I was impressed with his home-run hitting and the fact that he hit so many grand slams. I always felt, "All right, if he gets up, he might hit his grand slam." That was when I was about ten years old.

Rusty was popular but he doesn't really have the all-star status like some of the others, like a Tom Seaver, say. So I always went for underdogs. I always went for Bruce Boisclair, for some reason. He was just really cute, and I don't even know if he was that good. That was probably when I was eleven or twelve. It was like an obsession. Every time he came on TV I told my brothers to "Shut up."

The Mets had made the playoffs in 1989, and you had to dial a telephone number for tickets. That was the only way you could get any. Our family was having Sunday dinner, and the Mets said you could start calling at noon. I just kept clicking redial, redial, redial. I did it for hours and hours. When I couldn't do it anymore—if I had to go to the bathroom—I gave it to my father, and he would hit redial. If it was time to eat, I sat at the table with the phone, clicking redial. This went on for about five and a half hours. I finally got through. There was a limit of two tickets, so I got two. Of course, you don't get to pick when you want to go, which was fine with me.

Immediately after I got through, I called my brother Doug, who lived a few blocks away, and told him to try to call. He got tickets for the same game that we were going to. So I went with a guy I was seeing at the time, and Doug came with his wife. His wife and I decided we would make mimosas. She bought pink champagne and orange juice and the mix turned this really nasty color brown. It was disgusting. We got to the stadium parking lot where people were tailgating. We said real nicely, "Would you like some mimosa?" Everybody said, "Oh sure, all right." Then they asked us if we wanted a beer, and, of course, we were dying for a beer. So they gave us their Bud, and we gave them our brown stuff. One guy took a sip, and said, "It's not bad," but we could see he didn't want any. He covered his mouth and said to his buddy, "No, it's not bad."

When we sat down inside the stadium, it was cold, rainy, and nasty. We sat there for what must have been an hour and a half, when all of a sudden with the stroke of his arm, Chub Feeney comes out onto the field and calls the game. So, I've never gone to a playoff game. I had taken off from work that day. I couldn't take off the next day, too....

Strangely enough, my mother has a collection of prayer cards that are given at every Catholic funeral or at the funeral home and have a little prayer in the person's name and the dates when the person was born and died. What can you do with them? You can't throw them away? Well—guess who she has? Gil Hodges. Is that crazy?

The Yankees should eat Giambi's contract— it's low carb

THOSE BORDEN'S COUPONS WERE FREE AND THEY WERE WORTH EVERY PENNY

Joe Palmer

Joe Palmer, 49, works at the New York Times *during the day and is finishing work on a 500-page novel in his spare time. He has inside knowledge of the Mets organization because his sister was married to Lee Mazzilli for many years.*

We used to use the Borden's coupons. Remember the Borden's off the milk container? You'd collect 25 or 50 of them and present them at the gate, and they would let you in, and you could sit up in the upper deck. That was big. We used to go through garbage pails looking for empty Borden's milk cartons. A bunch of us guys would clip them, and we'd hop the subway. We used to put one coupon on the top and one on the bottom and the rest would be just regular cardboard in between. The ticket takers never checked them…we'd walk right in. We all did it. They'd think it was a whole thing full of coupons, and we'd walk right in. The first time we did it, it was a 'can't miss.' It worked every time. In the summer, when we were out of school, we'd go to 25-30 games. When the Mets were home, we'd go all the time. Elsie the Cow was never the same after that.

We ended up with box seats before the game was over. We would sneak down to the lower level. We'd have to change seats about 10 times when the ushers would catch us. Then, we'd separate, and one guy would go here, one guy would go there, and we'd all wind up in a box seat. All thanks to those Borden's coupons. I buy Borden's products to this day as a "thank you"…

We'd go to Bat Day. I got a couple of bats. Those bats weren't good because my father used to chase me around the neighborhood with them. That wasn't good. I've got some old memorabilia at home from the Mets—old yearbooks, a few signature baseballs. Today, the yearbooks cost $10-$12. I remember we paid 75 cents for them when I was a kid. We'd rip them apart and hang up some of the pages. I used to hang posters on my bedroom wall. I was into baseball cards big time. When we were kids, we used to flip them and play colors with them. If I had known what baseball cards would become.... My mother threw out shoeboxes of them.

New York is funny. A lot of times you get these fair-weather fans that go with the winners. In '69, the Mets turned this city upside down. A lot happened in '69. The Jets won the Super Bowl, the Knicks won the championship, and the Mets won the World Series. Man walked on the moon for the first time in '69. The Mets winning the World Series was bigger than man walking on the moon…in Brooklyn, anyway.

I realized the Mets might win when I saw that black cat walk across the Cub dugout. I was sitting there watching the game with my father, and he goes, "Look at that." I said, "What is that?" I didn't know that a black cat meant bad luck. He said, "The Mets are going to win." I said, "What are you talking about? They're 10 games out." He said, "They're going to catch the Cubs." I said, "You're crazy." My father used to drink beer when he was watching the games. My mother, who was Italian, used to keep bringing us food. He'd have a few of his buddies over. From 10…it went to 8 games…to 6 games behind. They made up 10 games in six weeks in the standing. Then when it came down to two games—one game…you just knew they were a team of destiny…

In the World Series, the Baltimore Orioles were loaded. The Mets had no shot—just like the Jets against the other Baltimore team earlier that year! The Mets took the Orioles in five games. I remember that like it was yesterday. Don Buford led off with a home run off Tom Seaver. You saw the catches they were making, Ron Swoboda, Tommy Agee. They couldn't lose. They were the team of destiny...The best Series catch you'll probably ever see, Swoboda's was twice as hard as the catch made by Willie Mays. They make a big deal out of Mays' catch, but the thing about Swoboda's catch was his whole body was extended. Then, who's Swoboda? He's just an average ballplayer, if that. The funny thing about Swoboda's catch was, I believe, when he made that catch, there were runners at first and second. The runners did not move up because he came up quick, and he came up throwing. Tom Seaver didn't win a game in that World Series.

Ralph Kiner was one of the most nostalgic commentators you'll ever find. He had some great stories. I used to watch *Kiner's Korner* all the time. After the game, he'd sit down and have *Kiner's Korner* in your living room. It gave me a good feeling, a comfortable feeling, watching how he related to the ballplayers, to show that the ballplayers were real people. When it came on I was just a kid, but I enjoyed watching it. He had all the old-timers on, guys like Seaver, Koosman, and those guys. It hasn't been on the air for at least 20 years....Bob Murphy was the best **PLAY-BY-PLAY ANNOUNCER**. Listening to him on the radio, he made you feel like you were watching TV. Then, there was Lindsey Nelson, with the plaid sports jackets. Those guys had color...Today, it's a lot different. Nothing is like it used to be. Baseball, today, is all about money. Back then, the players played 'cause they loved the game....

I liked Davey Johnson when he was the Mets manager. I guess 'cause he won the championship but, to me, he was a proven

> **Brent Musberger was the home plate umpire when TIM MCCARVER made his pro-baseball debut for Keokuk (IA) in the Midwest League in 1959.**

winner. It seems that every time the Mets got something good, they traded it off. They dismantled that '86 team. I couldn't stomach Valentine. He was a cantankerous, self-absorbed, a------. Mr. Right. I don't think he has good managerial skills either. The last time he was here, when they made that play-off run in 2000, a lot of his moves were idiotic. He was infatuated with John Franco, who, I think, stinks. I hated John Franco. He's a Brooklyn guy. He was overrated. He has tons of saves, more saves than any lefthander. But, he never knew when to call it quits. A couple of years later, the Mets were still in a play-off hunt, he used to get hit game-after-game-after game down the stretch—he cost them a play-off spot.

Billy Wagner and Delgado and these guys were a great addition…David Wright is going to be one of the best players in baseball. He's a great kid. He's disciplined. He's team-oriented. He's not pompous. I love the kid. If they put him in the third spot only, and they back him up with Delgado, you're gonna see this kid really do something…Beltran was a disappointment. I think Beltran got Beltran money because he peaked during the playoffs. He robbed major league baseball. He robbed the Mets big time. If he converts his dollars into pesos, what'll he have—10 billion?

First of all, the numbers in the American League and the numbers in the National League are two different things. Every day in the American League's inflated—the ballparks, the pitching isn't as strong. The National League is a pitchers' league. The American League is more of a hitters' league, especially with the DH. I don't like the DH because it takes the strategy out of the game…Another thing, **JOE TORRE** is the most overrated

JOE TORRE was player/manager of the Mets for 18 days in 1977. Since 1962, there have been four player/managers with Pete Rose (1984-1986) being the last….In 1935, there were nine player/managers.

manager I've ever seen in my life. In the National League, he couldn't win a game. Do you know that before he went to the Yankees, he was over 100 games under .500. Give him a two-hundred-million-dollar payroll, and all of a sudden, he's a Hall-of-Famer. He's what Steinbrenner wants. I've seen him in Atlanta. I've seen him with the Mets. I've seen him with the Cards. He's nothing special.

Mo Vaughn complained about sitting on the bench...how do you think the bench felt?

SHORT STORIES
FROM LONG MEMORIES

I went to Catholic school in Bethpage, Long Island, St. Martin of Tours, and I wore a blazer to school. I kept my Mets baseball cards in my pocket because I used to flip at school with the boys. It was hard, because the boys were on one side of the playground and the girls were on the other. I'd get in trouble if I were caught in the boys' line. One day, I came home from school and discovered that my mother had sent my blazer to the dry cleaners. I said, "Ma, did you check the pockets? My cards were in there?" She said, "Ah, who cares about that?" She didn't care. I was just a girl. If it had been my brother's cards, she would have cared. I thought, "Oh my God, I hope they send the cards back." Of course, they didn't. To this day, I never send any clothing to the cleaners without checking the pockets first.

———KATHY WAGNER, 57, Florida

My favorite Met to impersonate, which drove my best friend absolutely crazy, was Willie Montañez, the first baseman. Willie was a bit of a hot dog. He had so many mannerisms when he went up to the plate—adjusted his helmet, flexed his muscles. He was a lefty, and I was a right-handed batter. But we had to bat just like the players, and the great thing about Willie was his home-run trot, where after he hit the ball, as he approached each base, he would do this little stutter step. Just as he was about to hit the bag, he would leap into the air and touch it. And as he would leap in front of every bag and touch it, he would punch the top of his helmet with his left hand, just for a little dramatic effect. It was great. I thought it was the coolest thing. Of course, the opposing players on the field thought it was obnoxious. The older you get the more you realize this. Since I batted left-handed, the problem was I didn't hit too many home runs so I didn't have a chance to enjoy the trip very often. Occasionally if I hit a home run for one of my other players, I would incorporate the Montanez trot for them, just so I could get to do it.

——**KEVIN MARTINEZ**, 38, New Jersey, native

My five kids are sixteen, fourteen, twelve, five, and four. Every night before my kids go to bed, we all sing, "Meet the Mets," the song from the early sixties. And the deal is, all my nieces and nephews and my kids know, that at my funeral, they all have to get up and sing "Meet the Mets" before they shut the casket.

> MEET THE METS…MEET THE METS…
> Step right up and greet the Mets…
> Bring your kiddies, Bring your wife…
> Guaranteed to have the time of your life
> Because the Mets are really sockin' the ball.
> (Pop sound like bat hitting ball.)
> Knockin' those home runs over the wall.
> East Side, West Side, ev-'rybody's comin' down
> To meet the M-E-T-S, Mets, of New York town."

Copyright Ruth Roberts

——**CRAIG GANDOLFO**, 41, Long Island native

I went to the High School of Music and Art, and I was friends with a girl named Edith, who had very long hair. We used to call her "Cousin It" after the hairy character in the TV show, *The Addams Family.* We had to share a locker. We were both huge Mets fans, and up and down her side of the locker were pictures of Tom Seaver. Up and down my side of the locker were pictures of Tug McGraw.

I loved Tug McGraw. I liked the way he would take his glove at the end of the inning and whack it against his thigh on the way in to the dugout. It was his trademark move, and I just thought he was adorable. And he was good, too.

During the 1973 World Series, Edith and I had a class together. We were sitting in class, and she had a transistor radio in her bag by her feet. She had run the earphone up underneath her long hair so no one could see it. I knew she was listening to the World Series game, but nobody else in class knew. We both looked like we were paying attention to the teacher.

All of a sudden, Edith started whacking her book with her hand, shouting "Yes." Obviously, something good had happened, so, of course, I said "What?" She scrawled some note in her notebook that told me what had happened. The teacher kept looking over with an expression on his face like, "What the heck is going on?" But, he never figured out what we were doing.

——**DEBBIE ROSENBERG**, 47, Riverdale

When I was about eight years old, someone gave my dad a baseball, and he brought it home. I remember that it felt heavier than a normal baseball. I saw that it was signed by Joe DiMaggio, but who the heck was he, right? A Yankee. Somebody signed it separately in red pen, Marilyn Monroe. One day, my friends and I needed a baseball to play with, and this one had a black scuff mark on it, so I said, "What the hell." I don't think I had ever played with a real ball before so we used it, and of course it got torn, and we wound up wrapping electrical tape around it.

Last year my wife and I were watching the program, *Antiques Roadshow*. A woman brought **MARILYN MONROE** memorabilia, and the appraiser said, "This is very rare because it's a real Marilyn Monroe autograph. The way you can tell is that she always signed her name in red pen." I couldn't believe it. The value was several thousand dollars. Somewhere in the recycling heaven there is a piece of tape that had DiMaggio and Marilyn under it. I'll never forget that ball because it felt so heavy.

——**PATRICK HOGAN**, 47, Brooklyn

> To accentuate a wiggle in her walk, **MARILYN MONROE** would cut a quarter of an inch off one of her heels…. The combination on Monroe's jewelry box was 5-5-5, Joe DiMaggio's number.

Before I ever went to my first baseball game, I remember that when my family watched a game on television, when the National Anthem was sung, we'd all stand up in front of the TV just as though we were in the stadium. In 1966, I went to my very first baseball game. It was Ladies' Day at Yankee Stadium, and my mother took me and my older brother. Throughout my childhood, we only went to about one game a year, so it was a real event to go to a ballgame.

————CHARLIE ILARDI, 44, Riverdale

In 1986, the third game of the National League championship series was the Astros versus Mets at Shea. The Mets won it on a Lenny Dykstra home run in the bottom of the ninth. It was a Saturday day game. That night, I was going to a dance on a bus with a youth group. We were sitting in the car on the Van Wyck Expressway, and facing center field at Shea Stadium no more than four hours after this unbelievable ending to this unbelievable game. It was the first Mets playoff game at Shea since 1973 and I was jumping up and down sitting on the bus saying, "Yeow! Unbelievable! Len Dykstra is the greatest hero ever. Wally Backman set it up." It just got lost in all of the hair spray and mousse and raging hormones. The girls weren't looking at me at all. Let's just say I did not find the love of my life that night in Kew Gardens. Really, I had found the love of my life anyway—the Mets—and they had won the game that day.

————BARRY ABRAMS, 34, Television Executive

My mother is pretty religious. She prays to St. Jude, The Patron Saint of Lost Causes. In the Mets first season, she wrote a letter to them saying that she was praying to St. Jude for them. The Mets were horrible in **1962** and basically set the record for futility, so every time they won a game, she threw a dollar in a jar. At

> **After the first nine games in their inaugural season of 1962, the Mets were 9 ½ games out of first place.**

the end of the season, she mailed off the money to the St. Jude Foundation…a 20-buck bonanza for Danny Thomas.

The Mets liked my mother's letter, and they sent us complimentary seats. We celebrated my seventh birthday, on July 6, 1963, at Shea Stadium. It was my first major league baseball game. In 1963, the Mets were a little bit better but not much. I was already a Mets fan, though. That we went on my birthday as invited guests certainly anchored my fandom.

——STEVE ODELL, 50, Yonkers

Back in 1973, the year the Mets went to the World Series, I was about nine years old. As part of a Cub Scouts trip, we went to see a Mets game, which turned out to be on Old-Timers' Day. Of course in '73, the Mets didn't really have any old- timers yet, and so most of the old-timers were all Brooklyn Dodgers players.

My mom had come as a chaperone. She was a humongous Brooklyn Dodgers fan. She took me down to the field, where she talked to all the old Dodgers. Everybody was looking at us, saying, "Who's this woman?"

Well, my mom knew all these guys because she had grown up in the Hotel St. George in Brooklyn where a bunch of the Dodgers used to live during the baseball season. Her dad was a general during World War II. There were four children in the family, and the one closest to her in age was sixteen years older, so she was a late mistake. She lived at the hotel most of her childhood. On game days, the Dodger players like Preacher Roe, Duke Snider, and Pee Wee Reese, would ask my mom to baby-sit their kids. She knew the families really well.

When the other Cub Scouts saw my mother talking to them at the Mets game, that was my hook—I was "in" right there as a Mets fan. After all, the Dodgers weren't around anymore.

I didn't know at the time but my dad was a humongous Yankee fan. There were nine of us kids in the family and half chose the Yankees and half chose the Mets. We would listen to games on the radio, which kids today don't do. When the newspaper came out listing the games of the week, we would fight over and circle which game each person was gonna watch. If you knew the game was coming on at seven o'clock, you sat in front of the radio. We also had one little twelve-inch black-and-white TV, but we mostly listened to the radio.

——CRAIG GANDOLFO, 41

When I was twelve, I had a typical young teenager quandary on my hands. My friends and I had taken the twenty-minute Long Island Railroad trip from our home in Glen Cove, Long Island to Shea, and we had to make a specific train to go back. My parents couldn't pick us up at the station because they were both working, and they had arranged ahead of time for my Aunt Irene to pick us up. My aunt worked in the cosmetics counter at the nearby Lord & Taylor department store, so it was convenient for her to come and get us.

The game got tied up in the ninth inning, but I was telling my friends, "Okay, guys we've got to go." They were saying, "No, we can't go. Let's stay. We'll catch the next train." In the pre-cell phone era, changing arrangements wasn't easy. My friends and I stayed, and the Mets won that game in the eleventh inning.

My aunt didn't have children, and she wasn't used to this kind of duty. People like that tend to judge kids by how much they're disrupting their particular routine, and that's the way Aunt Irene acted. I've never seen anybody madder in my life when I walked back to her car at the main station. I don't know how long we made her wait at the station but I think it was about an hour and a half. She grudgingly gave all my friends and me a ride home, but the car trip was very quiet after I was sternly admonished about staying late at the game. When I got home, I got yelled at by everybody. I didn't get punished, but it was made known that I used poor judgment.

As a kid, it was hard to know what to do. Now, as an adult, I'm running out of games in about the seventh inning to beat the traffic. But I live outside Boston so that may have something to do with how small and uncomfortable the seats are in Fenway Park.

——ALEX WOYCIK, 46, Boston

My father's a Yankee fan and has been mad at me ever since I started rooting for the Mets. He's very angry. Every time we go to a ball game, he tells everyone in the stands that I'm a traitor. I always tell him it's his fault because he took me to Shea first. I didn't realize this until a few years ago when I was recalling my first memories of baseball. I clearly remembered getting on the 7 Train and going to a Yankee game. At first it didn't make any sense to me, but then I realized it was 1974 and the Yankees were playing at Shea because Yankee Stadium was being renovated.

The worst night, and the best night, of course, of our contentious sports relationship was Game 6 of the 1986 World Series. My father rode me endlessly. He was saying, "Oh, I can't believe the Mets had their opportunity and they blew it." He just went on and on for the three or four hours of the game. He rode me endlessly, saying things like, "Oh man, this is embarrassing to the city of New York." He was probably just teasing me, but he teases pretty well. He was really starting to get to me but I kept saying, "Just wait. Just wait." I didn't really believe that, but I knew that the only way I was going to survive the night was to say, "Just wait." And sure enough, Mookie came through for me.

——ROB STAUFFER, Queens native

My parents escaped Germany and the Holocaust and came to this country in 1940 when I was a year and a half old. I became a baseball fan in 1948, and after about two years, I turned my dad into a Dodger fan. He was an engineer, a very precise guy, and a compulsive record keeper. By the early 1950s, there were eight teams in the National League. My father would keep a graph in eight different colors, with the first-place team at the top. He would graph the daily progress of all eight teams, and end up with a season-long chart showing where they stood in relation to one another. I probably still have them somewhere because he never threw anything away. He died a few years ago at ninety-seven, and I haven't unpacked half his stuff.

——RALPH DANNHEISSER, 66, German-born, Manhattan raised

My late mother graduated from an all-girls high school in Manhattan in 1946. Underneath each girl's picture, it said "Favorite Pastime." All the other girls said things like "going shopping," "going to the movies," "going out with boys." My mother's was the only one that said, "going to baseball games."

When Shea Stadium opened in 1964, the World's Fair was being held across the street in Flushing Meadow Park. In retrospect, I can see that my mother was a genius because she would get me and my two older brothers up at the crack of dawn, haul us by subway out to the World's Fair and let us run around like idiots, go on the rides, throw things, and beat each other up. Then when we were good and tired, we would go across the street and get tickets for an afternoon game. She'd let us have junk to eat. We were too tired to cause any trouble, so this is how I got sucked in. It was pretty good because I got to eat hot dogs and ice cream.

———**DEBBIE ROSENBERG**, 47, Riverdale, N.Y.

Baseball was my baby-sitter. When we were kids, my mom and father divorced young. They'd put the ballgame on, and I'd watch the ballgame by myself when I was seven or eight years old. I just loved baseball. They weren't nearly as interested, and they were Yankee fans, anyway. Yankee fans are different 'cause they're always winning so they don't sweat the details. The way I see it, the most knowledgeable people were people who knew how to wait for a thing. You don't have to wait every year. When you do it, it's special year…

When I was a kid, I was a ballplayer and played for the Gil Hodges Little League. I wasn't just gonna be a major league ballplayer. I was going to be a Hall of Famer. Back in '69-'70, when the Mets were the big drawer in town, Gil Hodges Coney Island League was the most professional league. It had the fences, had the scoreboards, had night games with lights—in 1970, a long time ago. They're still happening now, but that was the opening. Any kid would have loved it in that league. You had to be a good ballplayer to get in there. Gil Hodges would show up on opening day. He'd throw the ball out. If you were a kid, that was the place to be…

In 1968, I was 10 years old, and my old man had taken me to a game. As my Dad went to go get some beers, Jerry Grote comes over and gives me a broken bat. I thought, "Oh my gosh!" I turned around and two kids 15-16 years old yanked it out of my hand. Dad came back with a beer in his hand. I said, "Where were you? Two kids took my bat." He said, "Don't worry. I'll get you a ball." About the middle of the game, **BILL MAZEROSKI** of the Pirates hits the ball, a pop-up. We had pretty good seats behind the dugout. The ball is up in the air. My old man is not much bigger than me, about 5'8". With a beer in one hand, he jumps up and catches the ball in his other hand. Beer spills over his head, he hands me the ball and says, "Now, shut up."

In '69, I got sent to summer camp in Peekskill, New York, which wasn't like camp is today. It was more like a discipline camp. You could be disciplined back then. There's no discipline today. I had a transistor radio in camp, and it kept me alive. It kept me in touch with things. I had to listen to the games all by myself because we weren't supposed to be having one there. Everything had to be out by nine o'clock—no fun. We went to bed with taps, and we woke up with reveille.

There was no TV at the camp so I was missing Woodstock. I was missing the 'moon walk.' I was missing the Mets through-out the summer. Here I am in summer camp, and I come home and my mom's got every newspaper from all the games—she had saved them for me. I started going through them. I remember the black cat night. I remember Seaver's near-perfect game with Jimmy Qualls and the whole bit. I liked Ken Boswell, who played second base. I liked to see the lucky bat.

—- **FRANK CIVITELLO**, Brooklyn

Hall of Fame Pitcher, Phil Niekro lost only one game in high school. The winning pitcher was **BILL MAZEROSKI**.

Two boys are playing hockey near the shore of the East River when one boy is attacked by a rabid Rottweiler. Thinking quickly, the other boy takes his stick and wedges it down the dog's collar and twists, breaking the dog's neck. A reporter from *The New York Times,* who is strolling by, sees the incident and rushes over to interview the boy. "Young Rangers Fan Saves Friend from Vicious Animal," he starts writing in his notebook.

"But I'm not a Rangers fan," the little hero replied.

"Sorry, since we are in Manhattan, I just assumed you were," said the reporter, and he began writing again. "Yankee Fan Rescues Friend from Horrific Attack," he continued writing in his notebook.

"I'm not a Yankee fan, either," the boy said.

"I assumed everyone in New York was either for the Rangers or the Yankees. What team do you root for?" the reporter asked.

"I'm a New York Mets fan," the child said.

The reporter started a new sheet in his notebook and wrote, "Little B-----d from Queens Kills Beloved Family Pet."

Chapter 2

Sweet Home Shea

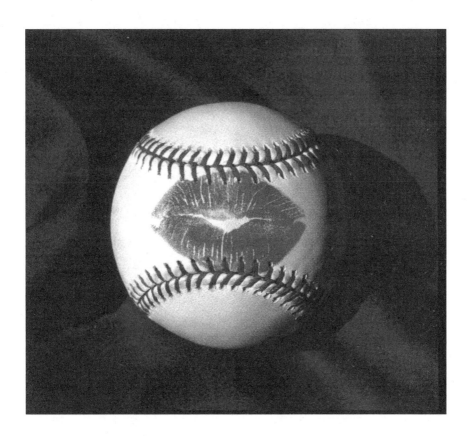

The Land of Ahs

SIGN OF THE TIMES

Karl Ehrhardt

From the year after Shea Stadium opened in 1964 until 1981, Karl Ehrhardt flashed signs of his own creation during exciting and dramatic game moments, earning him the appellation, "The Sign Man." Indeed, there isn't a Mets fan over the age of thirty for whom "The Sign Man" is not synonymous with the fun of the Mets experience. Mr. Ehrhardt, now living in Brooklyn, was never paid by the Mets, but his banners were so professional, their pithy phrases, like poetry, so perfect at capturing the home-game action, that it wasn't long before Mets TV cameramen knew to turn their cameras on him after a key play or hit. Wearing his recognizable black fedora, Ehrhardt was part of the show, no less than Ralph Kiner, on whose program (Kiner's Korner) he appeared numerous times. Ehrhardt also appeared on other television shows such as The Mike Douglas Show, *and was the subject of many New York newspaper articles.*

Now eighty, Karl Ehrhardt has not returned to Shea Stadium since 1981 when the Mets ownership pressed Ehrhardt to stop showing his growing repertoire of critical signs. Afterward, Ehrhardt destroyed most of his more than a thousand signs, though he kept about twenty "for old time's sake."

It all began in 1964 when a co-worker of mine, Charlie Taylor, and I said, "We've got to go to a game and we've got to hang something up—some kind of a sign." We were graphic artists with American Home Foods, and I was in the sales promotion department and did a lot of copy writing so making a sign came very naturally to me. We fabricated a sign two feet high and thirty feet long, made out of two panels, which we joined. On the sign, it said, "WELCOME TO GRANT'S TOMB." Donald Grant was the owner then. In those days, no one bothered you if you brought something to Shea. We had a seat up in the mezzanine, and we strung it out and hung it on the facing of the mezzanine on the third-base side.

We walked all the way over to the other side of the field, and you could read it from over there. It was as big as the numbers on the scoreboard. What happened was we hung it up before the game, and when the **"STAR-SPANGLED BANNER"** began to play, I stood up. With that, four maintenance men came running down the aisle and cut the sign from the mezzanine. They crumpled it up and ran back up where they had come from.

We were flabbergasted. We didn't know what the heck to do or say. So anyway, the "Star-Spangled Banner" was over, and we ran down to the press level, and we tried to see somebody from the newspapers. We got lucky. The door opened and out stepped a writer from Newsday, Steve Jacobson. I said, "You saw what happened?" He said, "Yeah, we wondered what was going on."

We explained the whole thing to him, and the next day he had a big article in the sports pages: CENSORSHIP AT SHEA. That's what got it started. After that newspaper article, we had to retaliate with something. So, we got a box seat the next homestand, and we made a sign that we held up. It was only about three feet long. It said, WE SCRIBBLE WHILE MATT BURNS. Matt Burns was the security guy. He was responsible for having that first sign torn down. Anyway, it went from there.

I made the banners out of black board stock. I would cut out white letters and affix them to the boards with glue. In the early days, they didn't have spray glue, so I would tape them on. Then, they came out with spray glue, and it was very simple. I would choose the signs to bring to games based on what team the Mets were playing. You're familiar with the game. You know what usually happens in certain situations. So, say the Mets were going to be playing against the Padres. You know who's on the team and who might be pitching, so you make a

Before Super Bowl XI, there was no **"NATIONAL ANTHEM."** Vikki Carr sang "America the Beautiful."

selection to suit that situation. Then you have to figure whether it's going to be a hitting game, or whether it's going to be a pitching game. You guess, and you make a selection on that basis. I'd take about fifty signs to a game, on average. I'd divide them in half, fold them, put them in a bag, and carry each bag under an arm. They weren't lightweight. They kept my arms in shape.

Very often, I'd get to a game, and I would use up three quarters of the signs in the first three innings and have nothing left for the rest of the game. Other times, I'd sit there the whole game and not use two or three of them because I'd misjudged and picked the wrong ones. I was right, though, seventy-five percent of the time.

A lot of my signs would cover both situations. I had 'pro' signs, 'con' signs, and 'individual' signs. I kept a filing system. I had little tabs on them with an identifying word, so I knew what the sign was, and I could pull them up without any trouble.

Ed Kranepool was one of my guys. I used to knock him good-naturedly. I hung the title on him of "SuperStiff." He got a little bit mad about it. We finally met one day, and I explained the whole thing to him, and we got real friendly. He appreciated it.

One of my favorites and a favorite of Ralph Kiner was a sign I had for when Jose Cardenal came up to bat. If he struck out, I had a sign that said, JOSE, CAN YOU SEE? Kiner thought that was great. He always told me, "That's a great sign."

I'll never forget Casey Stengel. He was known to talk and talk and talk a lot. We got real friendly. In 1973, the Mets went to Oakland for the World Series, and my wife and I went out there for it. We wound up in the same hotel where the Mets were staying. Saturday morning, I went down for breakfast and there was a big, long line in the lobby. I said, "What the heck is this?" I went around the corner, and there was Casey Stengel sitting on one of these old high-back chairs, like a king. He was signing autographs, and this was eight o'clock in the morning! I hadn't met him at that point. I said, "Well, I gotta get in line." When I reached him, he looked up and said, "Ah, the Sign Man." I said, "Yeah. Casey, it's so nice to meet you. Would you give me your autograph?" He said, "Surely." He took a piece of the hotel stationery and he wrote, "To the Sign Man, from Casey Stengel, Hall of Famer." I still have that. It's a wonderful memento.

Buddy Harrelson was another favorite of mine. He was always very generous with his comments to me. He loved what I did. He appreciated the fact that I was as honest as I could be, even though in some cases, it didn't set too well with the guys.

Sometimes, they'd come up to me and say something about a sign. Tom Seaver didn't think much of me at all. He more or less thought that I shouldn't be doing what I was doing. I never did criticize him, but he just didn't like what I was doing.

The fans loved my signs. Shea was amazing in the early days. The fans had been left high and dry when the Dodgers and Giants left so when Shea opened, everybody jumped in there. The Mets were so bad those early years. I used to go Friday and Tuesday nights. Every Friday night the place would be packed— and with a losing team! It was fantastic. We all got caught up in this atmosphere. We all just kept going and going. I would spend half the game signing autographs behind third base. The fans would come down to me and I'd write, "Karl Ehrhardt, Sign Man."

When I first started making the signs, I wrote on one side only, but when I would hold up a sign, guys would holler in the back, "Hey, turn around, I can't see what it says." So, I started making the front and back sides identical. By the time I stopped, I had about 1,200 of these banners made up, so 1,200 signs were really like 2,400 signs.

The more I had, the more difficult it became to select which fifty or so I would take to a game. I spent so much time making the selections for a particular game, trying as though through a crystal ball to predict what might happen, what type of game it would be.

The reason I stopped was I had a falling out with the front office. Earlier, I was more or less a cheerleader for the team. In the 1970s, the Mets started to go bad, and I started to knock the team with the signs. Like a guy would strike out, or a pitcher would throw a bad pitch, and I would put up a sign that said, YOU GET PAID FOR THIS? That kind of stuff. It started that if I went to a game, say, on a Tuesday night, on Wednesday afternoon at work I would get a phone call from the front office complaining about what I was doing. Different guys would call, but they'd all say the same thing. They'd say, "Take it easy. The guys are getting very upset. They see your signs. You're knocking us." I'd say, "Look, I call them the way I see them. The team's going bad and they need a little nudge."

Donald Grant was Chairman of the Board of the Mets. We got along very famously until this started. Then, it got to the point where I got so sick of these phone calls after every game I went to. You see, the guys from the front office would never come down to me in my seat and say, "Hey, cut it out," because they knew all the fans around me would get on them. So, they waited until the next day and called me on the phone at work. When I was cheerleading for them, it was fine, but when I was knocking them, they called me after every game. Finally I told them, "I'm gonna quit. I've had enough."

They never threatened to ban me from the ball park, but they implied as much. I beat them to the punch. I said, "I'm gonna quit. I've had enough of this harassment." At that time, there was a changing of the guard. Fred Wilpon and Nelson Doubleday bought the team from Donald Grant. Wilpon heard of my intention to quit so he gave me a call. He said, "Karl, you're a great fan. We need you here, and we don't want you to quit. Everything's gonna be different. I'll give you a place to change. I'll give you a parking spot. I'll even give you a seat. I won't harass you. You can say anything you want with your signs." So I said, "That's great."

So, naturally, I came back. This lasted for about five, six weeks, and then the same thing started all over again. I never got paid for anything and for years it had been one of my perks that I'd get invited to **OLD TIMERS' DAY**. I really looked forward to it. Well, in 1981, the year of the strike, they postponed the game until the last game of the season. After the game, I went up to the Diamond Club, as I did after most games, to have a drink and wait for the traffic to die down before I'd leave. When I went up there on this particular day, I saw all this stuff going on in the Diamond Club. I went to the door and said, "What's going on?" The guy at the door said, "Well, that's the Old Timers Dinner." I said, "That's wonderful. Am I on the list?" He said, "No, you're not."

They have glass doors there by the Diamond Club and I saw one of the top front-office guys. I said, "Hey, come out here a minute. What happened? I usually get invited to these things. That's one of the things I look forward to." He said, "Well, because of the strike, the dinner was delayed. As a result, we had so many more people that had to be invited, and we didn't have room for you." I said, "Come on, there's room for one more in this bunch."

One word led to another, and we started to holler at each other. A vice president came out, and he said, "Hey, what are you doing?" And blah, blah, blah. We got to talking real bad. A crowd

> During an **OLD TIMERS**' Game at Shea in the mid-60's, Bobby Thompson hit a Ralph Branca pitch on the fly into the left-field bullpen...Bobby Valentine married Ralph Branca's daughter.

gathered. One word led to another, and I said to him, "You know, I've had it with this club. I'm outta here. With all the effort I've put in for you guys, this is the thanks I get. I'm leaving. You'll never see me here again." That was in '81. I left, and I have never been back to Shea since. I was so aggravated over it.

When I got home, I couldn't sleep. I had these stacks of all these signs in the garage. Every time I pulled the car in or out, I'd be looking at them. Two months later, in the wintertime, I was out in the garage. I couldn't take it anymore. I took them to some dumpsters, and got rid of them. Twelve hundred of them. I saved about twenty.

I still make signs for the members of a business club I joined about eight years ago called The Bushwood Club. The members are businessmen, some retired, some still active. We meet twice a month for luncheons, and we celebrate the guys' birthdays. I'll make a big birthday sign, like 20" by 26" and bigger, and all the guys sign it and we present it to the guy with the birthday. Recently, we celebrated someone's 86th birthday. I made a big one that had a highway sign on a pole with the "86" on one part, and "Happy Birthday" on another. The line I wrote was, "Get Your Kicks on Route 86." We have two or three guys every meeting that have birthdays. Around Christmas time, we had about seven at one time. So, it keeps me busy. It keeps the old graphic juices going.

I still find myself thinking about signs when I watch a ballgame. I see a situation, and I say, "Boy, I have the right sign for this situation." I transport myself mentally, and I'm there, holding up a sign. I used to spend so much time thinking about new signs for certain situations or certain players. It was just fifteen years of fun and games. I still miss it. You enjoy the notoriety. You become a minor celebrity. The ego needs whetting all the time, and you miss that. Remember that Gene Raskin/Mary Hopkins song, "Those Were the Days"? "Those were the days, my friend, we thought they'd never end."

'69
THE YEAR THE METS TURNED NEW YORK UPSIDE DOWN

Patrick Hogan

Forty-seven-year-old Brooklyn resident Patrick Hogan is now in his fifth decade of attending Met games. His wife, Ann, has ESP ... or maybe ESPN?

In 1964, my Dad took me to my first baseball game. The Mets were playing the **COLT 45s**. I remember that Bordens was the Mets' sponsor. They led a cow around that was supposed to be "Elsie the Cow."

The Mets were not just bad. They were historically miserable. There was no comparison to anybody. I guess the **ST. LOUIS BROWNS**, who in 1898 lost 111 games, once had a season comparable to the Mets. Year after year, the Mets were just terrible. They were still my team—I was just a kid. When the Mets were playing on the West Coast, I used to go to sleep listening to their games on a little transistor radio earphone. It was like my nursery stories. I

> The public address announcer for the Astros (**COLT '45s**) in 1962 was anchorman, Dan Rather. John Forsythe, the actor, was the P.A. announcer for the Brooklyn Dodgers in 1937 and 1938.

> All six games of the 1944 World Series were played at Sportsman's Park in **ST. LOUIS**. The rival managers— Luke Sewell of the Browns and Billy Southworth of the Cardinals—shared a one-bedroom apartment during the season... never expecting both teams to be in town at the same time.

didn't know back then, but I never have rooted for a favorite. You're identified by your religion and the teams you root for.

In 1968, we decided to enter a Mets Banner Day parade. It used to be a really big deal. Now, it's almost a curiosity. The banner parade between games used to take an hour and a half. About the seventh inning of a doubleheader, all the participants would be called down. There would be ten or fifteen thousand people. It was a happening. They had well known people, such as newspaper illustrators, who acted as judges. Prizes were items like color TVs, which were a big deal in 1968. You'd parade outside behind the bullpens, and they'd open up the centerfield fence, and you'd walk out on the field along the warning track and then along the outside foul line so you weren't really walking on the grass. There would be a guy out there as you walked in, and he would tell you which way to walk. If you were holding a banner that was really good, he would direct you to walk over by the judges.

My friends, Duane, Carlos, and myself, decided to make a big banner. Carlos was really artistic. I was just glad to walk on the field and hold it up, but he was trying to win the contest, and he drew a beautiful banner. What we didn't realize was that Carlos, though he drew very well, was color-blind. He drew the Mets logo perfectly, with the skyline looking over the 59th Street Bridge. But instead of coloring it blue and orange, he used red and purple.

We got to the ball park, and the other guy and I were looking at each other like, "God, we've got to walk out on the field with this?" It was really an elaborate thing. Mr. Met was drawn perfectly, drawn to scale on this bed sheet but he's all the wrong colors. Carlos kept telling us, "These are the colors," so we didn't say anything to him. It was our only chance to walk on the field. The banner was about fourteen feet long. Somebody sewed two bed sheets together, and it took three of us to hold it. My friend and I said to each other, "At least, we get to be on the field."

The banner was mostly folded up as we walked out. On the field, the part showing first was the Mets logo, which was drawn and colored in beautifully, except that it's purple and red. The funny thing was, there was a guy who lived across the street from us, Elliott, who either was color-blind also, or who was bagged at the time he looked at our banner. He said, "That's the most beautiful thing I've ever seen." My friend and I each got to thinking, "Maybe I'm just seeing the wrong colors." Obviously, our banner didn't win....

One of the weirder memories I have was when Tom Seaver was traded. I was not in a great place in my life at that point. I was so upset that I wound up going on a bender. I came out of it after a couple of days and was sitting in a saloon. I heard somebody say, "Seaver is warming up in the bullpen." I said to myself, "Oh my God. I have imagined the whole thing." They just had gotten a guy in a trade named Paul Siebert, and I thought the announcer had said "Seaver."

I can still see Seaver in my mind. I can still see his motion. It was absolutely perfect, compact. His right knee always scraped the ground as he was getting ready for his delivery. He got down so low that literally one of the ways he would judge his mechanics is that he would check the dirt stain on his knee. If you stop-framed the photographs, you would ask how can a human being throw from this position. He didn't throw directly overhand. He threw three-quarters overhand, which is the reason he never threw a really good curve ball. He threw a great slider. He was the first player who I knew lifted weights.

This year for my wedding anniversary a friend of mine gave me a Seaver autographed baseball. I have no autographs. I don't collect them. When I saw that it said, "Tom Seaver, R-O-Y [Rookie of the Year], '67," I can't describe the feeling I had. It was like being a kid again....

In the spring of 1986, before the season started, my wife, who knows nothing about sports, said, "The Mets and the Red Sox are gonna play each other in the World Series. It's gonna go seven games, and the Mets are gonna win." So in the sixth game, it was horrible. The Mets were losing. I like the Red Sox, but I love the Mets. It was ripping me up.

They were losing by two runs in the bottom of the tenth inning. There were two outs, nobody on. I always remember Annie, my wife, coming and sitting on the floor, taking my hand, and saying, "Relax. I told you it's gonna go seven games, and the Mets are gonna win." Beside the Mets losing, I was thinking of all the Yankee fans who were gonna be harping on me the next day. At the time, George Steinbrenner was a guest columnist for the *New York Post*. After the Mets lost the first two games, his line was, "Welcome to the Big Leagues," so now I was really mad.

The back window of my house is a block from a major boulevard here in Brooklyn. After the Mets won the sixth game, car horns were honking, people were just screaming. The Mets hadn't even won the Series yet, but they had come back that day. When the Mets did win the Series—after what Annie had said—it was just so weird.

MARRIAGES ARE MADE IN HEAVEN...
SO ARE THUNDER AND LIGHTNING

Michael Polvino

Michael Polvino, 49, is one of a panel of "experts" who appear on the Mets program, Pohl Position, *a Queens-based, public cable television show named for host Howie Pohl. Reared in a Buffalo suburb, Michael's initial attraction to the Mets was rooted in sibling competition and hatred for the Yankees.*

My older brother, Tony, was a Yankee fan so I became a Dodger fan. My brother and I spent an entire childhood just needling each other. That's probably why my parents are gray.

My brother watched the Yankees all the time on TV or listened to them on the radio. By the time I woke up, it was 1963, and the Dodgers were playing the Yankees in the World Series. He always bragged about how the Yankees were "gonna kill those guys." I said, "Nah." And of course, my team won 4-0, and I was very happy about that.

I did not become a Mets fan until 1978 when I moved from a suburb of Buffalo, where I grew up, to New York City. The only reason I moved to New York was that there were two baseball teams here. The Mets were really bad, but there would never be a way I would embrace the Yankees because I hate the Yankees. I've always liked the National League baseball better anyway. I like the game better. So I said, "I live in New York. I'm a Mets fan."

Tony and I would go to games together—either to Yankee Stadium or to Shea. It was cheap enough. You could go to a game for four or five bucks back then. I'd have to sit there and take it every time. He would say, "Your team stinks," or "My team is great!" And there was nothing I could say about it.

I lived within walking distance of Shea Stadium, so I would walk to the games. It was a lot safer than driving after drinking a few beers. One night, the Mets were playing the **PHILLIES** and they were getting beat up, as usual. It was a nice summer night, and the Mets got a rally going. There were down by two or three runs when they loaded up the bases with two outs, and up strides Frank Taveras.

So few fans would show up. In those days we all had our own section. The guy in the next section over screamed, "OH NO! NOT YOU!" And the guy in the next section over from him turned around and looked at him and said, "They got nine 'Oh no, not you's' in the lineup."

We used to joke that Bob Murphy, on the radio, should say "Hey, Mets fans, if you're driving by Shea, drop in…there are still plenty of good sections available."

Since nobody went to games back in the seventies, streaking was very popular. It was like, "Who cares? Nobody saw you." Or, somebody would jump out of the stands and run along the first-base line, and the cops would stop them. It wasn't because there was a lull in the action—there was no action for there to be a lull. This is a team where your clean-up hitter hits .282 with eleven RBIs, and four hundred at bats. People would just be amused and say, "Hey, look at that fool out there." You would go to a game back then just because you couldn't get to the beach. You would go because there'd be a cool breeze at Shea, and

> **P.K. Wrigley and Milton Hershey were bitter business rivals. When Wrigley bought the Chicago Cubs, Hershey tried to buy the Philadelphia PHILLIES… and sell chocolate gum. Hershey failed in both efforts.**

guys would bring you beers. It was like watching your son play basketball when he's seven. You know you're not going to see him score sixty points. You know he's not going to dunk the ball. You know there's gonna be ridiculous stuff happening all over, but you love him and want to support him.

Why did I love the Mets? I had just decided they were going to be my team. When you are a baseball fan, that's what you do. "This is my team." You don't hop from winner to winner. That's traditional in baseball. Whatever team is the one you choose to root for, you follow them where ever you live. People in Pittsburgh are Mets fans. People in Kansas City are Mets fans. That is, if they were originally Mets fans.

I used to go to every home game, though now I can only afford to go to about half that, about forty a season. I still have my ticket from Anthony Young's twenty-third consecutive loss as a starting pitcher, which is a record from 1993. He lost eleven straight games at home, and I hit all his losses that year.

Back then, by the time a game was over, there'd be about eight-thousand really friendly people left in the stands. Anthony Young ended up being traded to the Cubs after the '93 season, and then he fell off the face of the earth. He had really good stuff: a live fastball, good curve ball, good control, but no focus. Not a clue as to what was happening once he hit the rubber.

He would go out to the mound, blow hitters away, and then try and fool them with the same pitch. He'd usually give up about eight runs in the fifth inning—end of game. It didn't matter where he pitched, whether he started the game or whether he came in as relief.

There would be a headline in the paper, "Anthony Young Starts Tomorrow." Twenty consecutive losses, twenty-one consecutive losses, great stuff, twenty-two losses. Several of my friends said, "Let's go to the game." The Mets just kept throwing him out there because he had great stuff. He'd look like a God for four innings. Every game, we'd go and say, "You know, he looks really, really good today. He's out there. He's in total control. He's got one walk in four innings. This is great. We're gonna pick up a win. We're gonna pick up a game in the standings. This is nice. He's gonna win this game."

We'd get up for a beer. We'd come back. We'd look up at the scoreboard. We'd say, "Why are there men on second and third?" They get three runs in. By the end of the year, the fans were just amused by it. You know the feeling you have when you know you've done something wrong. You're fourteen. You're just waiting for your parents to find out. But in the meantime, you're joking around with your friend about how your parents are going to kill you. That's the feeling you had with Anthony Young pitching. It was like, "You know, it's really fun right now, but it's not gonna last. It's gonna roll over and die."

And that's what would happen. The Mets would end up losing those games like 8-3. The Mets had a solid team so they'd probably be ahead after four innings, but the sky would fall in—in the middle of the game—every time, with this guy on the mound. It didn't matter. There was no avoiding it. Chalk it up. Be prepared. Say what you want about Anthony Young. Frankly, "Loser" comes to mind.

My older brother, the Yankees fan, ended up marrying a very lovely young lady whose only fault in life was that she was a **RED SOX** fan. It's not a really good way to start a marriage, a Red Sox fan married to a Yankee fan. Every September in their house was very tense. They were both rabid. They would

> **The Sam Malone character in *Cheers* was patterned after former RED SOX pitcher, Bill Lee...Bill Lee once demanded number 337 from the Boston Red Sox because 337, upside down, spells Lee's last name.**

scream at each other. They wouldn't watch ball games in the same room. They lived in Connecticut so they could get both teams on television. Beverly would watch in one room. Tony would watch in a different room, or he would go out to a bar and watch the Yankees. They couldn't be around each other. They'd start screaming at each other.

As much as a Yankee fan as Tony was, he had never been to a World Series game. I had season tickets to the Mets, and when you have season tickets, you get World Series tickets. So in 1986 I invited my brother. I said, "Come down to the city. Game Two. Let's watch the World Series." We went and had a wonderful time. We were sitting in nosebleed country. He had mixed emotions. It was a wonderful game, and he really enjoyed it, but the Red Sox won. So he was a little depressed when he went home. How many Yankee fans really root for the Red Sox? None!

The next day, he called me up at work and said, "You know, thanks. That was a fabulous experience, one of the best nights of my life. But I'm paying for it today. You should have heard Beverly on the way home. 'You get to go to the game, and I don't. The Yankees aren't even playing. My Red Sox are there. My Red Sox win. My Red Sox are gonna win the World Series for the first time in a million years, and YOU get to go to the game?'" And on, and on, and on. This went on for three days. Finally, my brother called up and said, "Is there any way that you have tickets for any other games?" I said, "Yes, I do have tickets for Game 6. I'll tell you what. Come on down. Stay at the house, and I'll take Beverly and we'll go to the game."

So my brother's wife and I went to the game. Beverly was a well-mannered woman, and she knew not to get really crazy, surrounded by fifty-five thousand Mets fans. But as the tenth inning unfolded—it was a cold night, crisp—the Red Sox went up two runs. She couldn't contain herself. She was standing. She was cheering. Of course, you'd look around and you'd see all eight Red Sox fans in the stadium because they were the only ones moving. Everybody else was just stone-cold silent.

We were all the way up in Section 27, Row M, about ten rows from the top, all the way down right field, up near the lights. Come the bottom of the tenth, one out, two outs, the Stadium was so quiet, you could hear the Red Sox players in the dugout, "We've got it. You got the champagne? I can't believe this. We're finally gonna do it." We could hear them from up there. That's how quiet the stadium was. It was unbelievable.

And then, slowly, but surely the Mets started coming back—a single here, a single there. They brought in Calvin Schiraldi, who did absolutely nothing. Now my sister-in-law was feeling, "I've got this game in the bag. This is great." She started jumping up and down—happy, happy, happy. Single by single, base by base, she began to sag a little bit. She said, "Now, they are not going to blow this. This is too good to be true. I'm gonna win. Finally, it's been almost seventy years. They are not going to blow this, are they?"

Well, the Red Sox brought in Bob Stanley, and half the stadium looked at each other going, "Wild pitch, wild pitch." My sister-in-law at this point had taken off her coat, taken off her gloves, and was screaming, "Throw strikes, throw a strike." She totally lost sense of where exactly she was. I was sidling away. I didn't want to get hit with anything if the Mets fans started throwing things at her. I said something like, "Hey, this is great. This is like the greatest comeback I've ever seen." When the Mets tied the game up, she was stone-cold silent. She said, "They can't lose this game."

The next thing you know, Buckner let the ball go between his legs. The Mets won the game. Everybody was jumping up and down. I almost broke my ankle when I jumped up, and landed on the seat in front of me. We were high-fiving. We were hugging. I turned around to my sister-in-law, and she was just standing there.

There was one tear coming down her cheek, and I said, "Sweetheart, I'm so sorry—NOT!" She looked at me and said in just a little, small voice, "It's okay."

On the car ride home, there was total silence. Not a word was said. When we got home, my brother did his best to console her. She put up a brave front, but she wouldn't say anything. I asked her, "You okay?" She nodded. I said "Do you guys want to stay over?" She said, "No, we want to go home." They had a two-hour drive back to Hartford, Connecticut. My brother didn't say a word, got her in the car, and they went home.

At two o'clock in the morning, I got a phone call, and in a cheery voice my brother said, "Thank you. That was the best gift I've gotten since I got married. They lost." I said, "You're my brother. She's your wife. Pick your sides as you see fit."

They divorced a year later. It was a fair divorce. She got the inside of the house, he got the outside...and the luggage.

Some people think that Steinbrenner is the backbone of the Yankees. i wouldn't put him that high.

I HATE PEOPLE WHO ARE LATE...
LIKE THE LATE BOB MOOSE

Seth Magalaner

Originally from Greenwich Village, Seattle-based Fox Sports producer Seth Magalaner, 46, has seen the underbelly of professional baseball in a career in sports television broadcasting. As a result, the Mets of his youth are likely the last time sports attained a state of perfection.

I became a Mets fan in 1969 and remained a fan throughout the seventies despite all rational impulse to the contrary. You can't live through a year like '69 and then just decide to change because the Yankees get good.

I had a charmed introduction to the game of baseball. My first game was June 27, 1969. My dad took me, and the Mets lost to the **PIRATES**. The second game we went to was Bob Moose's no-hitter against the Mets. It was September 20 of that year. The third game we went to was the third game of the playoffs when Nolan Ryan came out of the bullpen and shut the Braves down and the Mets won the pennant. That's a pretty amazing introduction to any sport and one of the reasons why I think I just remained a Mets fan. Those three games are sort of my touchstone for baseball, particularly the last two. To have the second game you go to be a no-hitter—even when the home team loses, is pretty amazing.

At that Bob Moose no-hitter, I didn't get an official game program, but it was an election year, and a guy named Sanford

The Pittsburgh **PIRATES** was also the name of a National Hockey League team for five seasons in the 1920s.

Garolick, who was New York City Mayor John Lindsay's police commissioner, was running for City Council. He had souvenir score cards that he was giving out that said, "Vote for Sandy Garolick." I kept score for the no-hitter—I still have it, in my nine-year-old penciled handwriting—and in 1973 when I was thirteen, I brought it with me to Shea to a game when the Pirates were playing the Mets. I went down to the visitors' dugout, hoping I could get the scorecard signed by Bob Moose.

I waved the program, hoping that Bob Moose would come out of the dugout. Of course, he didn't. He was down in the bullpen, down the tunnel. A rookie named Richie Zisk was standing a few feet away. He turned out to be pretty famous later on, but at that time he was probably the last guy on the bench. I waved the program at him, "Mr. Zisk. Mr. Zisk." He came over and I got his autograph. Then I said, "I have this program from Bob Moose's no-hitter. Is there any way you could take it down to the clubhouse and get him to sign it for me?" Richie Zisk took the program and came back about five minutes later with it signed. I think Bob Moose signed it, though it could have been signed by Joe the Clubhouse Guy. But it was signed, and I thought that was great for a ball player to go and do that. The tragic part is that three years later I read that Bob Moose died in a car accident at the age of twenty-nine.

AN empty CAb pulled
Up iN front of Shea
Stadium ANd Art Howe
Got out

YOU CAN'T GO TO HEAVEN
UNLESS YOU'RE A METS FAN

Marc Beck

Marc Beck is a 33-year-old marketing executive who is a longtime Mets season package holder.

I became a full-fledged Mets fan the day in 1983 the Mets traded Neil Allen for Keith Hernandez, who had always been one of my favorite players.

What Keith Hernandez said at the end of the sixteen-inning Game 6 of the 1986 NLCS against the Houston Astros, one of the greatest games in history, was so incredible. The Mets had come back from 3-0 down in the top of the ninth to tie it. They took a 4-3 lead in the fourteenth, only to blow it, but then they went up 7-4 in the sixteenth inning. Then, the Astros got back two runs. Jesse Orosco, the Mets pitcher, had thrown three or four innings of relief and his arm was about to fall off. There was a meeting at the mound with the winning run on second and the tying run on third, and Keith ran into the huddle—this was in the newspaper the next day—and said, "If you throw anything but a curve ball, I'm gonna kill you." So sure enough, Orosco threw three curve balls and struck out Kevin Bass to end the series. The Mets won and went on to the World Series. Keith Hernandez always did that kind of stuff. He ran that team.

My folks actually let me take the day off from school so I could get Hernandez to sign a copy of the book he wrote after the 1985 season called *If At First*. Unfortunately, each person in line only got about two seconds with the guy. I got his signature, then went home and read the book. I still have it. A couple of years ago, he did a signing at the Mets Clubhouse Shop. I wore my Keith

Hernandez jersey, and he actually posed for a photo with me wearing the jersey. Afterward, because he had touched my shirt, I said to him, "Now, I feel like the shirt has been blessed."...

The first batter of the inning, Benny Agbayani, hit the game-winning **HOME RUN**. In the midst of the celebration, we were just jumping on top of everybody. I picked up the kid, gave her a hug, and said, "Promise me that every time you come to Shea, you'll wear this hat, and you can keep it." She said "Okay."...

This is how my friends think: During the fifteen-inning game against the Braves in 1999, the Robin Ventura grand slam-grand single, we were sitting out in right field in the "greens" under the covered seats. Somebody left to go to the bathroom so I moved over a couple of seats to talk to someone. While I was sitting there, apparently a flock of pigeons appeared and sat up in the rafters above us. One of the pigeons did his business on my back! I heard a bunch of groans from behind me. I turned my shoulder and saw everybody looking up. I'm like, "Oh, s---" Somebody said, "That's supposedly good luck." And that's when the Mets won that game in fifteen innings. Everybody said, "Hey, you see. We told you."

Actor Charlie Sheen has always dreamed of catching a HOME RUN ball. For an Angels game in Anaheim, he bought every seat in the left-field pavilion to ensure that he would get his coveted home run ball. The tickets cost him $6,000...there were no home runs hit during that game.

METS FEVER:
NO CURE

Dr. Joe Gomez

Dr. Joe Gomez, following in the footsteps of his father, a surgeon, is an internist in Rochester, New York. Dr. Gomez was raised in Bayonne.

For the final game of the 1986 playoffs, my dad had one ticket up in the second to last row of the upper deck, and then he had one field-level seat. You couldn't get into the field level unless you had a field-level seat, so we had this scam worked out where we would enter the restaurant right at field level. Everybody could get in through one door, but you could only get out to field level if you had a field-level ticket. My dad and I had this elaborate ruse where he would slip out first, put his head down so the guard at the door wouldn't see him, and then I would walk backwards toward the fence, slip my hand in between the fence, get the ticket from him and use the stub to enter the field level. By Game 7, my dad had been doing this for two weeks.

The same **USHER** worked the first-base line section every night, and my dad would see the guy and give him kind of a wink. The guy would put his hand out and my father would

> The most famous usher currently is Ed Hoffman, "The Singing <u>USHER</u>," at Edison Field in Anaheim. His son, Glenn, managed the Dodgers and another son, Trevor, holds the record for most saves with one team (Padres).

throw probably a couple of hundred dollars into the guy's palm. The usher would escort us to the back, right behind field level, so we were actually standing with our backs against the wall. About thirty people would be doing the exact same thing. They knew the usher. They paid him. The guy probably made a fortune during the Series. After every half inning, he would come over, and knowing exactly who paid him, he would point and say to the people who didn't, "You're out of here. You're out of here." And everybody else would stay.

People ask me about the excitement of the game and what it felt like to be at Game 7. An October night in New York can be pretty cold. Everybody was packed so tightly. People started out the night wearing winter coats, but by the third inning, your coat was at your feet, and you just sunk into the warmth of the crowd. My dad is a head and neck surgeon, so he's very, very protective of his hands, and would always wear gloves if there was the slightest chill in the air. He never went near sharp objects, because he was always afraid of hurting his hands, which are his livelihood.

In the middle of the game, the fans started chanting, "We will— we will rock you!" I remember whenever they did the "We Will Rock You" song, everybody would either stamp their feet or clap their hands. Here was my dad—a guy who would get upset whenever you would shake his hand too hard—banging his hands on the back wall of the field level which we were standing against. His fist was just pounding away at the concrete. It was absolutely phenomenal how caught up in the moment he was. We finished the game, and we stayed in the stadium for two hours. We smoked cigars while the players drank champagne on the pitcher's mound. It was unbelievable.

Growing up, Tom Seaver was always mentioned as the idol, though we were really a little too young to have the 1969 guys—Seaver, Jerry Koosman, Gary Gentry—as our baseball models. We were in first or second grade when the Mets beat the Reds so we rooted for Bud Harrelson while everybody just wanted to NOT be Pete Rose. Everybody was anti-Pete Rose then. You fooled around being funky when kids pretended they were fighting and you did Buddy Harrelson versus **PETE ROSE**. My friends and I had those matches in the living room with my brothers. It never got rough, but sometimes Buddy Harrelson beat Pete Rose up in the simulated fights unlike the real.

A friend used to ask, "Can you name ten major league players named after a flower?" Everyone would get Pete Rose. Then the guy would say, "Don't forget the nine pansies playin' for the Yankees..."

When I was in my freshman year at college in 1985, it was before cable, so if you wanted to watch a game that wasn't on local television, you had to make an effort to go somewhere. In Washington D.C., eight or nine of us hardcore Mets fans found a Mets bar in the middle of the city, called Poor Robert's. It was on Connecticut Avenue, about halfway across the city, a good cab ride away. The owner must have had a satellite dish because the Mets games were shown on the big TV screen.

This was a hardcore Mets fans' bar. It was the home of the Ed Kranepool Fan Club. It was great. I have no idea how we found this out, but we were freshmen and nobody had cars, so we would all pile into a cab and go down there for the playoffs. This was the year the Mets were chasing the Cardinals. It was the second to last series, might have been the last series of the season. We had to win. We were three games back with three to play, so we had to win all three.

PETE ROSE is enshrined in the Summit County (Ohio) Boxing Hall of Fame.

The guys from the Ed Kranepool Fan Club were great. My friends and I were by far the youngest people in the bar. We were of age because D.C. had an eighteen drinking age limit at the time, but these guys were forty-fifty years old. I don't know where they came from or what they were doing. I have no idea what the relation to Ed Kranepool was, but they had "Ed Kranepool, our hero," on the walls, along with a lot of other Mets stuff.

It's over 20 years later and I can tell you that at least three times a year, somebody is pulling out the Mets highlight reel at parties or at Thanksgiving dinner. Obviously, we can recite the tape word for word, with accents. It's great. We haven't had that much to talk about until this year, but the Mets take you to a different level. It's something that all of us just kind of live and die by.

Anna Benson has the right to remain silent but doesn't have the ability.

VANDALS DID $400 DAMAGE TO SHEA...THEY TORE IT DOWN

Frank Civitello

Frankie Civitello, 49, is a carpenter in Brooklyn and a life-long Mets expert. At one time, he was a towering figure in the Wagner College social circles.

I heard a story that the Mets took the blue from the Dodgers and the orange from the Giants when they left New York. When they were gone, to bring the Mets back as a National League team, they did that in honor of the old National League teams. I think that's a true story. I heard it from an old-timer who was around back in that time. I'd buy that.

In '73, my friends said, "Let's go to the game." This is the game with the Bud Harrelson—Pete Rose. I'm looking at the picture right now on the wall. I have the ticket right here— loge—right over the left-field dugout. Things start to happen. My friend's cousin takes a 7-Up bottle and he flips it down to Clay Carroll in the bullpen. Everything starts happening that inning. Pete Rose is coming out to left-field, and fans are throwing golf balls at him. He picks one up and throws it back. The next day, our picture—the four of us—is in the *New York Post*. Here we are cutting out of school, and our picture is there in a very noticeable way. There were no truant officers at Brooklyn Tech, and no one was watching, so we didn't get in trouble. I was doomed to be a Met fan my whole life....

To get those Yankee-Mets tickets, you've got to wait in line in February. You have to go early in the morning, like at four o'clock, and wait eight or nine hours. But, it's worth it, 'cause you get the tickets. But, before the last couple of years, you could get eight tickets a person. Now, they've cut it back to only four. I still get my 24 tickets.

A couple of years back; it was the opening night of the movie *The Hulk* and the first night of the Yankees-Mets series. I was always a big "Hulk" guy. When I was younger, I dressed up as The Hulk and would run around the neighborhood. Back then, I had some muscles. I had purple pants. I told myself, at age 45, I was a little bit past it, but I had to do it one more time for old-times sake. In the eighth inning, the Mets were losing 5-0. I told one guy out of the 24 what I was up to. I went out back and got myself green. I had my pants. I came running out down the exit. Everyone was looking at me. The fans were stunned at first. I didn't go on the field. People were telling me to run on the field. I said, "Are you crazy? I'll be jailed like this." I ran down the aisle, towards home. Everybody is getting into it. It's a sellout. I was being careful. I didn't want to knock anyone over. I could hear my friends in the loge as I'm running toward the plate. They were in section one behind home plate, so they're pretty loud. I started to go down the right field line, just like if you're going to go out on the field, just under the stadium. Then, the security says, "Okay, here he is." They were looking for me. I was no threat. I wasn't drinking. They said, "We got the Hulk." I said, "No. You've got the Incredible Hulk." He said, "You wait here. The captain wants to talk to you." They had me stay there and kids were coming over taking pictures of me. The security guy comes over, and he's really p----- off. He was a New York City cop and the head of security at Shea. He says, "What the h---'s the matter with you? Have you got nothing better to do?" I said, "The Mets are losing 5-0. I'm having a little fun, and the people are loving it." He said, "Get this guy out." So, he threw me out. I said, "Let me go back to my seat and get my ticket." They walk me back to my seat. Everybody is yelling, screaming, cheering. We all got up and left—all 24 of us. I'm so glad I did that. That was the best retiring from The Hulk. I'm done with that....

We used to do Banner Days when we were kids. There were two really hard things about Banner Days. One time, we were playing the Phillies. In the seventh inning, you had to go down under the stadium to get ready. One year, back in the early seventies, the game was tied, and they played *11-extra-innings*, so we're underneath the stadium for 11-innings. That's your whole day. Another time, the Pirates were here. Both games got rained out. They made us walk up and down the field with the banners. All the paint is running off, and it's a total mess. Cartoonist Bill Gallo was the judge. He's standing there, and you have to walk by him. He looks at you, he shakes his head, and you've got to walk by. A couple of weeks go by, and I see my banner there in his cartoon in the *Daily News*. I see my words from my banner, so I write a letter to the *Daily News* and say, "How come my banner was good enough for you to use, but I didn't get anything from it." Gallo answered, "You want to know something—great minds work alike." And, he sent me two tickets to the next game.

That year was a year when everybody was hurt. I had Mr. Met painted in the middle. I said something like, "Don't worry. We'll play through this." I had guys all painted up with crutches and bandages. I've forgotten just what I said, but it was good enough for Bill Gallo.

It was a two-man banner. I used to have to beg my brothers to do it with me because you needed another person. All the kids in the neighborhood resented it. No one would come out. No one would even be a part of that banner day thing. My mom loved it. She made it a point that if we were going to get to go to one game per year, it was always going to be the Banner Day. We did it for six or seven years as a family, which was nice. But, without doubleheaders, it just doesn't happen these days.

Little things like that were just part of being a Met fan. When they had the song "Meet The Mets," it's not the time of your life anymore. It's different being at the ballpark now. They're not looking to keep you there for things like that. If they could, they'd keep you there forever, to make money, but I guess they're not making money on it.

A new stadium? Well, why not? The Reds, Pirates and Phillies stadiums have all gone. Let's face it, Shea is nothing to look at, but I don't really care. If you're going to give me one, I'll take it, but…. I really will keep that place. I don't see the need for it. I know it doesn't matter, and people always want these retro stadiums. If it comes, it comes, but I don't want to spend money on it. If it comes down to that, use the money wiser. We don't need a new stadium here.

Current management? The game has changed a lot, and I don't get as excited about it anymore, especially since they bring in guys like Matsui. Here's a guy who came from Japan. In his contract, he had to play shortstop. Now, you've got your bonus baby coming up. You've got to move him. I don't understand it. Matsui *has* to play shortstop, according to his contract. If you're gonna play ball, you have to play shortstop. I don't get it. Who discovered this guy? It's just the Mets looking for a bargain. That's one of their things.

Great. Even the Yankee fans like Willie Randolph. But, then, last year, he tries to make a double switch and he screws up. He can't manage in the National League. I didn't like Bobby Valentine. I thought he was more 'look at me.' Bobby Valentine once said, "I won't let the game situation dictate the way I manage my team." What the hell's a manager supposed to do? That's what he does. He was his own self. I thought, when they got Art Howe, they were doing better, but he just sat back too long, too.

It's a shame Anna Benson wasn't still here so she could comment on Keith Hernandez's "women in the dugout" remarks.

QUICK HITS AND INTERESTING BITS

There's a guy at Shea who sits to my left behind home plate nearer to the third-base side. He comes by himself all the time. He always wears a suit, a light-colored cowboy hat and a Lone Ranger mask. He never takes the mask off. When they play the "William Tell Overture," he gets up and runs up and down the aisle. I've been tempted to talk to him, and I think sometime I will go up to him and say, "Who are you?" He has to be a season-ticket holder. Every once in a blue moon, you'll see him on Diamond Vision, usually going up and down the aisle.

——TOMMY FLYNN, 54, Queens

The night before the first opening game ever at Shea Stadium, the Mets allowed two or three hundred people in to walk around the field. I remember walking around and seeing that the sod wasn't set in yet. One banner I especially remember from an early Banner Day was really terrific. It said, "To error is Metsian, to forgive is a Mets fan."

——EDDIE MILLER, 71, Bronx and Florida

Both my son and daughter worked as vendors at Shea Stadium. They were there the night of the big blackout in 1977, and it happened to be my son's first night to work. My wife and I drove down to the stadium and waited in the parking lot. Thousands of people were pouring out. My son was only thirteen so my wife was very upset, but it turned out okay. He had one of those rock n' roll T-shirts on that was sparkly, and we caught him in the headlights.

——JOE BROSTEK, 73, New York City, Queens

My dad took us to a Mets game when I was about fifteen years old. I don't even remember who they were playing. My dad was all ticked off because he wanted to go home, but he couldn't find us anywhere and he was furious. Back in those days, nobody was ever at Shea and we were walking around the stadium. Suddenly, Bob Bailor, the Mets infielder, hit a foul ball and my buddy grabbed the back of my belt as I leaned over the mezzanine wall with my feet off the ground. He was holding me like this as I caught the ball. My dad, who had been frantically looking for me, looked up on the Diamond Vision and saw me holding this ball up above my head like it was *Ferris Bueller's Day Off*. He didn't know whether to hug me because he had found me and I caught the ball or scream at me because he couldn't find me.

——CRAIG GANDOLFO, 41

I went to every Mets Opening Day for about fifteen years. One of my great visual memories is the final day of the 1963 season when the Mets had had another horrific season. At the Polo Grounds, where the Mets played until Shea was built for the '64 season, the clubhouse wasn't under the stands. It was out in center field, so at the end of the game the players and coaches had to walk across centerfield to the clubhouse. I remember Casey—he had to be in his mid-seventies then—kinda doddering across by himself. At one moment, beyond second base, he turned and sort of looked at the crowd and tipped his hat and just kept going.

——BILL BERENSMANN, 68, Brooklyn, Upstate New York

Early in the 1987 season, I did something that became a trademark for myself. I always thought it would be fun if I could get total strangers around me involved in the game. In April and May, Rafael Santana hit three home runs. I remember saying to my friends, "Look, it's Rafael 'Babe' Santana. I'm going to call him 'Babe' Santana. You know why I'm going to call him Babe Santana? Because he's hit three home runs now, and he wears number three. It's just like the 'Babe,' and with the pinstripes the Mets wear—it's like the 'Babe' is out there." I kept going on for the whole game. At the end of the game, the man in front of me stood up and shook my hand and said, "I just have to thank you." I said, "Why?" He said, "Because I'm a New Yorker, but I've lived in Los Angeles for the last twenty years. At Dodger Stadium, nobody talks."

I say it's because none of the Los Angeles fans know what's going on. They have their transistor radios with the ear pieces tuned in to Vin Scully who patiently explains to them what's going on in the ball game. No one interacts. No one even reacts. Everyone just sits quietly, passively, which is alien to the New York sports experience. So after that, I said, "Well, that's it then. I'll make a fool of myself, and it's okay."

——CHARLIE ILARDI, 44, Riverdale

Just in case the Mets need a rally, one of us in our group always brings to Shea a flask of tequila. We sneak it in by putting it in an empty bottle of contact lens solution. Somebody brings the little mini-Dixie Cups and another person brings the contact lens solution bottle. Sometimes the tequila doesn't taste quite right, but I think that's part of the fun. I think to be a true Mets fan, there's something not quite right with you to begin with. One Tequila, Two Tequila, Three Tequila, Floor

——MARC BECK, 33, Queens

A couple of years ago I was at Shea Stadium for Irish Night. It was quite an experience. The crowd before the game and for the first three or four innings is about the loudest you could ever imagine. They are enthusiastic. They are cheering. They're just having a great time. Then usually around the fourth inning, you notice that the stadium becomes remarkably quiet, for the number of people that are there. I'm part Irish so I'm not denigrating them. It just seems like a significant amount of the fan base is really too drunk to even function at that point.

I will never forget this one Irish Night. They ran out of beer! How can a baseball stadium actually run out of beer? I don't know if they were out across the entire stadium, but I know for a fact they ran out on the mezzanine level. I had been standing in line for a couple of beers, and when I turned around to talk to my friend a few people back in line, the guy right behind me almost bumped into me. I couldn't believe who it was—James Doohan, "Scotty" from Star Trek. I'm a big Star Trek fan so I thought, "Wow, Scotty!" He was there with some Irish guy who had sung some songs before the game. I was so excited, and I wanted to shake his hand. The middle finger on his one hand had been shot off on **D-DAY**. I looked down, and I had a beer in each hand. I thought, "Where can I put them?" Then, I looked over at him, and he had a beer in each hand, too. He must have been about seventy years old at the time, and he had two beers in his hands! We both just looked at each other, and I said, "Well, it's really great to meet you." He said, "Likewise."

——CRAIG NARDI, 43, Connecticut and Florida

One summer afternoon, my friend, Jon Spoelstra, and I were in the players' lounge waiting for Tug and Swoboda to come out. We had to talk to them about something and then we headed to our car. Spoelstra, who later became president and/or general manager of the Portland Trail Blazers, Denver Nuggets and New Jersey Nets, grew up in Detroit. We are walking toward our car. These young kids had seen us come out of the players' lounge, and they're begging us for autographs. We kept telling them we weren't players. Finally, Spoelstra grew tired of all the pestering, took their autograph pads and signed, "Wayne Comer." Only a dedicated baseball fan would know that Wayne Comer was a very obscure reserve outfielder with the Detroit Tigers in those days. Everyone of those kids knew who Comer was. Each of those kids were thrilled with their "Wayne Comer" autograph; not one of the kids questioned why "Comer" was in New York.

—DICK FOX, retired, Florida and Cape Cod

The first American to jump off the boats at the **D-DAY** invasion was James Arness of "Gunsmoke" fame. At 6' 7", he was the tallest man on the first ship and the ship's captain wanted to test how deep the water was.

In the '69 World Series, when the TV cameras panned in from centerfield, you had that shot in to home plate when the pitcher is pitching and you could watch the catcher. There was this lady who was sitting in one of the box seats right behind home plate. She would do this windmill kind of thing with her arms to try and distract the pitchers of the Orioles. It was the most amazing thing you've ever seen because of the way the camera honed in on the shot—it's taking a shot from center field, and you have the pitcher's back, and then you could see the catcher and umpire and the hitter. This lady always seemed to get on camera with this 'windmill.' It was the funniest thing. She was just sitting there windmilling.

———RON LICHTENSTEIN, 57, Hermosa Beach, California

One of my early fantastic memories of Met games happened in 1984, Dwight Gooden's rookie year, when my aunt got tickets for us in the blue seats, which are in the second tier at Shea, right behind the plate. It turned out to be the game where Dwight Gooden threw the one-hitter that should have been the no-hitter, except that Ray Knight was not given an error on a ground ball hit by Ryne Sandberg of the Cubs. When they gave Sandberg a hit, the mood at Shea went beyond electric. It was crazy.

The play happened late. Nobody ever talks when a pitcher's throwing a no-hitter, but we all were just sitting there like, "This is ridiculous," because Gooden was a rookie. Short of a play-off game, that was about the most excitement I've ever seen at Shea. No Mets pitcher has thrown a no-hitter, ever. And I believe that in all of Major League Baseball, with the exception of the Colorado Rockies expansion team in 1993, only the San Diego Padres have never had a pitcher throw a no-hitter. Even the Florida Marlins had a no-hitter thrown by Al Leiter.

———BARRY ABRAMS, ESPN Producer

A lot of people will say they were present for some great championship moment. Although there were only fifty thousand people in Shea Stadium, a million people in New York will say they were there when Lenny Dykstra hit his home run to win a playoff game, or when the ball went through Bill Buckner's legs. You don't generally have people vying to say, "Oh yeah, I was there in 1981 when they came back after the strike." I was one of the thousand in the stands who were so starved for baseball, so starved for the Mets, that I went out to see an exhibition game there.

The strike had ended unexpectedly. Tickets went on sale so suddenly that during the first exhibition night game against the Toronto Blue Jays there were less than a thousand fans in the stadium. It was Ellis Valentine's first game with the Mets.

Everyone there was such a dedicated Mets fan and baseball fan. These were people who had a horrible summer because of the strike. They were really excited that baseball was being played again. Rusty Staub came to bat, and the Mets fans particularly loved Rusty Staub. People went crazy. I remember a concessionaire came down and said something disparaging about Rusty. I thought people were gonna lynch him right there.

I wish I could come up with some terribly funny story about Mets games, but I'm afraid they fit more in the category of general stories like when you take a kid out to Opening Day when Tom Seaver comes back to pitch for the Mets. It was such a moment of excitement for people, and you ask the kid what he remembers most, and he says, "When we went to the bathroom after the game, you peed next to a guy who had big legs." That was my godson. He has to be in his mid-thirties now. He'd be very embarrassed if he knew I was telling that story.

——**T.J. ELLIOT**, 53, Educational Testing Service

There's always a battle between being an analyst and being a fan. In my heart of hearts, the fan wins every time. But there's also something to be said for being able to be analytical about it. You can have much more intelligent conversations about baseball if you can be analytical. When you, as a fan, try to have a conversation with someone who is a fan of another team, it just descends into gobbledygook.

I hadn't first planned on going to the Mets game that turned out to be the first sporting event in New York held after September 11. I thought it would be too much of a hassle with all the extra security. But the more I thought about it, the more I wanted to be at Shea. The team, complete with their tribute hats, swept Pittsburgh during the week and they were playing with a lot of emotion. I was so glad to see them scrape back into the race because it was such a pleasant distraction from everything that was happening in New York. I went out that Friday before to the Mets Clubhouse Store, a few blocks from my office and bought a group of tickets.

The lines were crazy, of course. The game start time was moved back to accommodate the delay in people being seated. There was a buzz among the crowd, a shared feeling of being someplace special, like a playoff game, but different. It was a little more quiet, more emotional. But this is New York, so there were still a few rowdies, even that night. There was a fight in our section, and everyone cheered as the combatants were carted out. I remember thinking, "How much of a flaming jerk do you have to be to get into a fight on a night like this?"

The ceremonies were so surreal, so amazing. The pipers choked everybody up. Diana Ross sang, "God Bless America." There was something I thought I'd never see—Rudy Giuliani, Yankee fan number one, actually getting cheered and chanted for at Shea Stadium. We all joined in.

But the moment of silence was the most stirring. I swear, 40,000 baseball fans have never been so quiet, ever. That night, the usual pennants that fly above Shea were replaced with American flags. The only sound in my section of the stadium came from the flag above us, flapping in that ever-present upper deck breeze.

The game itself is a bit of a blur—until the end, anyway. Bruce Chen started and looked great. The Mets were quiet on offense against the Braves' Jason Marquis, not even one of their studs. The place had a World Series-like atmosphere. I remember Liza Minelli sang, "New York, New York" during the seventh inning stretch. The Braves got a run in the eighth off John

Franco, and I was really scared they were going to lose. I still don't understand why I was so upset by this prospect. I mean, how silly to be genuinely concerned about the outcome of a ballgame in the face of all the country had been through. Except I really did care. It was as though the pennant were riding on it.

In the bottom of the eighth inning, Steve Karsay was pitching to Edgardo Alfonzo, and it looked like he had struck him out. But the ump called the pitch ball four and here comes Mike Piazza. I remember Ed praying for Piazza to hit a home run in what eventually became the last out of the Subway Series. Well, this time, I wanted a home run even more. I don't remember what the count was when it happened. But I remember clearly that it was one of those Piazza "no-doubt-about-it" monster shots, this one to centerfield. And I just went absolutely bonkers, jumping up and down as if they had just won a playoff game. Armando Benitez came in in the ninth and shut the door.

In that game, on that night, there was just no way they were going to lose.

——**PETER FORNATALE**, 33, Long Island

About ten years ago, the Mets began holding an official International Week where every night would be dedicated to a different ethnic group: Italian night, Dominican night, Polish night, German night…The first year they held it, they didn't have a Jewish night. I was not among those who created the uproar, but there must have been a big one because I read in one of the local sports pages that the Mets were defending their decision by saying, "Well, we didn't have a Jewish night because for 'International Night' the group has to have a nation. Jewish isn't really an ethnic group…"

There must have been a continued uproar because the following year, sure enough, there was a Jewish Night during International Week. Several of us in the group are Jewish, and some aren't, like Manny Morales, who we consider an "honorary Jew." I went out and bought a Mets yarmulke in honor of the occasion. I was wearing it as we entered the ballpark, and we had a good laugh about it.

The game was a tight, one-run affair. By the ninth inning, the Mets were up by a run. Now they brought in John Franco to close the game. In our group, we refer to John **FRANCO**, the alleged relief pitcher, as the 'F' word. When he makes a relief appearance, it's not just a relief appearance, it's an adventure. He does not understand the meaning of a one-two-three inning. He has like a one-two-five inning. He has to put a couple of guys on base to make the game a little more interesting. A couple of years ago, when Franco would come in to take his warmups, I would turn to the assembled section and ask everyone to guess how many base runners he would allow on base. We have one guy, Sam Gonzalez, who sits next to us on the Saturday plan. Every once in a while he would say zero because he likes to be hopeful. Everybody guessed one, two—we had a little sweepstakes to see who would be right. It was almost never "zero." When Franco pitched a one, two, three inning, this is cause for fainting.

When Franco came out of the bullpen with the score 1-0 Mets, we were all saying, "Please don't do this to us. Anything but this guy." He came in, and with his usual shtick, he got two outs right away. Then, he proceeded to walk everyone and his grandmother, or the other team got these little dribbler hits and the next thing you know the bases were loaded. Now everyone in the stadium was on their feet trying to cheer John Franco on to get this last bloody out. As we stood up, Manny said to me, "Give me that Mets yarmulke." He put it on and began to daven. He's now chanting with a Yiddish accent. Franco got the last out.

——DEBBIE ROSENBERG, 47, Riverdale, N.Y.

Former Met, Matt **FRANCO** is the cousin of actor Kurt Russell. Russell had a decent minor league career until he "blew out" his knee in a Double-A ball…Elvis Presley's cousin, Kirk Presley, a pitcher from Tupelo, Mississippi, was the Mets first-round draft choice in 1993. Presley was 8-10 in five seasons before injuries sidelined him permanently.

Chapter 3

Fandemonium

IT WAS IN THE *NEW YORK TIMES*, SO, HELL, FOR ALL I KNOW, IT COULD BE TRUE

Ruth Roberts

Ruth Roberts has been the Mets' Queen for a Day every day since the team's first season. That is because Ruth, now in her seventies, and co-wrote the music and lyrics that every Mets fan knows and loves, "MEET THE METS—MEET THE METS—step right up and greet the Mets..." Ruth and her partner, Bill Katz, have nearly five hundred published songs to their credit, including the Dean Martin song, "All in a Night's Work", and "Mailman, Bring Me No More Blues", recorded by Buddy Holly and John Lennon.

Though Ruth's partnership with Jimmy Dean and Katz' death in 1998 resulted in the Number One song on the charts for sixty-five weeks, "The First Thing Every Morning and The Last Thing Every Night," Ruth says "Meet the Mets" remains at the very top of her personal chart of favorites. Today, still living in Port Chester, New York, where she was raised, Ruth Roberts' company, Michael Brent Publications, Inc., produces music for elementary school-age children. In a way, "Meet the Mets" began the same way four decades ago, when Ruth's young son, a budding Mets fan, nagged his mother and "Uncle Bill" in the dire hope of getting a season ticket.

My son Michael was about twelve. He practically hit Bill and me on the head to write the song. He wouldn't give up. Bill and I thought it would be easier to give in to him. Eventually, it had come out in the press that the winner of a Mets song-writing contest would get a season pass to the games. Bill and I didn't know about the contest, though we later found out that everybody in town wanted to write a song for the New York Mets. We only wrote it because Michael kept saying, "Oh, come on, Ma. I can get a season's pass. Come on Bill." You know how kids are.

It took us a day or two to write the song. We got off to a good start. Sometimes you get off to a wrong start with a song, but we got off right. We didn't start at the top, but in the middle, where the lyrics go, "Bring your kiddies, bring your wife, guaranteed to have the time of your life." The rest seemed to write itself. We made a simple demo with just a bass guitar and piano. Neither Bill nor I had a singing voice, so we hired a singer. We submitted the song to the Mets in November, 1961.

When we got the phone call from someone in the Mets press corps telling us we won, I thought it was a joke. I was about to hang up. I said, "Who'd you say this is?" Then, my husband recognized the fellow's name and said, "Wait, don't hang up. I know that guy. He's in the sports section." The man said, "You came in first place." The Mets wanted to meet us, and they wanted to make a big recording. We wound up getting a lot of beer from the beer sponsor. Cases and cases of beer were sent to our house, and we gave it to the neighborhood. It was fun. The whole neighborhood was rooting for the Mets by then.

The Mets changed only one part, which is very unusual—usually everybody wants to put something in—but the only change came from Mrs. Payson, the owner. She loved the **SONG** and the New York Times wrote an article about how she walked around the house singing the song. She liked the colors orange and blue so she had somebody call us and say, "Please, your song is beautiful. We don't want to mess it up, but could you put orange and blue some place in the song?" That actually was the first time the team was associated with orange and blue. It was very easy to do. Bill and I wrote a little passage that goes,

> **Phil Rizzuto is the only baseball person to earn a Gold Record...his game-calling was in the background of Meat Loaf's "Paradise by the Dashboard Lights..." Rizzuto was the first-ever mystery guest on *What's My Line*.**

"…and the fans are true to the orange and blue so hurry up and come on down."

The master recording of "Meet the Mets" was made on March 1, 1963. It was introduced to the public on Saturday, March 9, 1963. Bill, my son Michael, and I were all given passes because the Mets were so pleased with the song.

The responses to the song were great. People went crazy. They called; they wrote; they wanted a copy. The Mets made the arrangements for us to release the song as a record. We had a big recording session with a professional orchestra. That's what you hear on the CD. Our company has a Web site, michaelbrent.com, which is not linked to the Mets, but is intended for music students. People write all the time and request copies of the sheet **MUSIC** and the CD. Generally though, people write to the Mets and they refer them to us.

All these years, the Mets people have been so pleasantly wonderful to me. They have honored the song frequently. On September 15, 1996, they held New York Mets CD Day. Everybody who came to the ball park got a free CD of "Meet the Mets." I threw out the first ball. They took my picture with Bobby Valentine, who had just become the Mets' manager. My son, Michael, is real proud, and I have two grandchildren. They live in California and all fly in every time the Mets decide to do something about the song. Though Bill and I originally wrote "Meet the Mets" so Michael could get one season's pass, the Mets always find room for me when I want to go to the ball

The band, Pearl Jam, was originally named Mookie Blaylock, after the NBA player, and they recorded their first album, "Ten" under that name. Blaylock's uniform number was "10." In 1992, the band Mookie Blaylock changed their name to Pearl Jam, after a hallucinogenic concoction made by lead singer Eddie Vedder's great-grandmother, Pearl.

park. For many years, there were five of us: my husband, Bill, Michael, a friend, and me. It was a very neighborly, fun kind of activity, and I wish kids who are growing up now could get the same kind of feeling.

I don't think people really know me or know Bill, but what they know is the song. They sing it as they walk to the stadium. They sing it as they leave. The just like singing it. If Bill and I were ever in New York riding in a taxi, the cabbie somehow found out we had written the song and he would never take a nickel. Couples have walked down the isle to "Meet the Mets," rather than "The Wedding March," especially if they met at Shea Stadium. When Bill and I were writing the song over forty years ago, my neighbor across the street had a baby. He was about a year and a half old and hadn't learned how to speak yet. Because he could hear us singing the song over and over as we wrote it, the first words he ever spoke were, "Meet the Mets." His mother still reminds us all the time that we taught her son to speak. "Meet the Mets" ranks right up there as one of the favorite songs I've written. I wish everyone could have the pleasure I've gotten from having co-written that song.

I ran into a Yankee fan today. then, I backed up and ran into him again.

MARK BOMBACK: GREAT NAME... IF YOU'RE PLAYING SCRABBLE

Vin Cannamela

Vin Cannamela was born in Metuchen, New Jersey, almost forty years ago. He is a veteran film producer for ESPN.

I never remember not being a Mets fan. They're the one team I still live and die with. My first memory was watching the 1969 World Series. I was a few weeks shy of my fourth birthday. I was born with a heart condition commonly known as "blue baby." I had surgery, and I remember being brought home and laid on the couch. The couch was facing the TV and the World Series was on, so that's my first memory of the Mets.

Then, when I was six—almost seven—in May 1972, I had to have heart surgery again. My parents tell me the operation lasted a long time, five or six hours. Afterward, the ballgame was on television in the recovery room. The Mets were playing the St. Louis Cardinals, and the Mets won 2-1 even though they were up against **BOB GIBSON**, the premier pitcher in those days. My parents were worried that my mind would be affected when I woke up from the anesthesia. Evidently, my first words when I finally woke up were, "Did the Mets win?" My dad said, "Yes, they did." I asked him, "Who was the winning pitcher?"

> **BOB GIBSON** played basketball with the Harlem Globetrotters several off-seasons...In 1972, Bill Cosby signed a lifetime contract with the Globetrotters for one dollar per year. In 1986, the Globetrotters gave him a nickel raise. Cosby made several appearances with the team and is an honorary member of the Basketball Hall of Fame.

He said, "Number 39." I said, "Oh, Gary Gentry." My dad said he knew then that my mind was okay.

Because of my heart condition, I was a fairly sedentary kid. My father would watch all the Mets games on television and I began to memorize every Mets player, his uniform number, his position, his batting averages, etc. Tom Seaver was my favorite. I always told people my name was "Vincent Joseph George Thomas Seaver Cannamela." It was a long name so I said it was shortened to "Vin." I wore a number 41 jersey all the time, and I had pictures of him all over my bedroom. Seaver could do no wrong in my eyes.

As we grew older, the Mets were our fascination. We would make up these Whiffle Ball leagues. We would each have four teams in our league. We'd make up a schedule, and we'd each have a Mets team. We would have a draft, and of course, we were the players. This was in the seventies when the Mets were at their depths. So here we were having a draft with this team that barely was a major league team, but we didn't care. We just loved these guys. I would have Sergio Ferrer as my third pick because he was short just like me, and I liked him. He was a fun name to say—Sergio Ferrer, a typical Met of that era. So we had all these great games and we would **IMITATE** Bob Murphy.

When you're nine and ten, you don't realize how horrible your team is because it's the team you identify with. They're just your team and you want to root for them, and you watch every game you can, and you listen on the radio. The fact that they're twenty-two games out of first place—well, yeah, that's tough, but they're your team. I think as great as 1986 was, what made it

Rich Eisen, a former ESPN anchorman, is now the host of the NFL Channel. He worked his way through college as a comedian. Part of his act was reading *Letters to Penthouse* while IMITATING Howard Cosell's voice.

even more special was that we had gone through all those barren years. If you're going to go through barren years, it's good to do it when you're ten and eleven years old.

My father didn't have the patience for the Mets that Kevin and I did, and he would make fun of them. He wouldn't sit there when they were twenty-two games out. He used to say "The potentials, the potentials," because of all the runners they would leave on base.

Then he would have names for these guys. Roy Staiger became "Roy Stinker." Ray Searage became "Ray Sewage." It didn't make me mad. It was funny. If he became a little too critical, I would say, "All right, give it up dad, we know they're bad." But it was funny. He made up this song for Mark Bomback that he'd sing while we watched the games on TV. "Bomback, Bomback, go bom-back to the minor leagues."

The 1986 World Series was played when I was a junior in college. A bunch of us were Mets fans—everyone knew I was a Met fan—and some people called our group the "Oh S---ts," because we would walk in our apartment, and they'd say, "Oh s---, they're here."

The apartment had windows that faced a main thoroughfare, and lots of people would pass by the window every day on their way to the cafeteria or a dormitory. As soon as we moved in, I took masking tape and put up a sign that read, "Mets Magic Number," and every day I would reduce the number by whatever games the Mets had to go—first during playoffs, then the National League Championships, and then until they won the World Series. I put up a sign that said "Mets: NL East Champs," then I took out the word "East" and put "NL Champs." I had a lot riding on the Mets winning the world championship.

For me, part of Hernandez's appeal was that he had been part of the enemy playing for St. Louis. He had killed the Mets for so many years. I think there was always something about Gary Carter where you questioned his sincerity. Of course, the more you know about him, the more you realize that he really is that way, that he really is a happy guy. But Hernandez, for me, was so much more what baseball was about because he was cerebral and intense. I love defense, and the guy could obviously play first base with the best of them.

I married a Red Sox fan from Boston, but she's learned to be a Mets fan. Our wedding had a baseball theme. Instead of giving a number to each table, guests were assigned to a different "stadium." Of course, my dad was seated at "Shea Stadium," and my wife's family was at "Fenway." We didn't give a name to our table, but we put a Red Sox batting helmet in front of her place setting and a Mets helmet in front of mine.

there's a 50% chance that the Mets are going to win the World Series this year but there's only a 1% chance of that happening.

MR. DeMILLE, I'M READY FOR MY CLOSE UP NOW

Tommy Flynn

Tommy Flynn, 51, is a retired Flushing cop who has made "fan" commercials for the Mets. Flynn and his wife, Joan, consider Shea Stadium their second home.

My uncles, Bobby, Brendan, and Jerry, took us to Mets games all the time when I was a kid. The Yankees-Mets rivalry was pretty intense with my uncles and they passed it right on to me. From day one after the Mets were born, when Casey Stengel was the first manager, the Mets were mine and my brothers' love. My room was filled with Mets stuff and clippings, which I pinned to a big bulletin board. My brothers and I collected baseball cards like everybody did. It was easy to trade for Mets cards because at that time people wanted to give Mets cards away. Frank Thomas was one of our favorites. We sent him a get-well card one time when he was in the hospital. When the TV announcer said, "Frank Thomas thanks all the fans who sent him the get-well cards," we felt like he was talking to us. Another favorite of ours was Ron Hunt, number 33, a real scrappy second baseman. He hugged the plate and never backed off. He held the major league record for being **HIT BY PITCHES**.

The night the Mets beat St. Louis to clinch the division in 1973, we had gone out onto the field and formed two big circles

> **Don Drysdale said his most important PITCH was his second knockdown one because it told the hitter that the first knockdown pitch was not a mistake.**

around the pitcher's mound. Jane Jarvis was playing, *"Dream the Impossible Dream."* This was just before my nineteenth birthday. I was a cop and got off work at midnight and went to pick up my brother Robert and a friend. We drove out to Shea because tickets were going on sale at nine o'clock the next morning. We slept overnight in sleeping bags at one of ticket booths to get playoff tickets. It was very chilly that night, and I had zipped the bag around my head. I heard my brother and his friend laughing. I unzipped the bag, and there was a pigeon sitting on me looking me eye-to-eye. That ended up being good luck because we got good seats.

It was a big party that night in '73 when the Mets won their division. The fans didn't tear the ground up that time because some of the playoff games were going to be played at Shea. As I was leaving the stadium through the bullpen fence, a young man from Avis car rental handed out red bumper stickers with white lettering in a white circle, which said, "We try harder. So do our New York Mets." My friends and I had borrowed my father's station wagon to go to the game and we put them all over the car—front, side, top, back, windows. Later, we couldn't peel some of them off. My father really read us the riot act. Because of this, he only let me take his car to Game 5 of the World Series....

I have lots of unique memorabilia, like the '69Mets record album that contains songs about New York sung by the Mets players. I've kept ticket stubs from every playoff game I've ever been to. I bought season tickets in 1983, two seats, that I share with my brothers, and in 1986 I actually had a bird's eye view of Bill Buckner missing that ground ball. When Seaver first came back from playing for Cincinnati, I went with a bunch of guys from my precinct, the 77th. That was the year the movie *"E.T."* came out. I printed up a huge banner that I unfurled from the railing of our upper deck box that said, "G.T. CAME HOME."

The photo wasn't printed anywhere, but was mentioned in a **_SPORTS ILLUSTRATED_** article the following week.

I have field dirt left from '69 in a Mason jar in a locked strongbox. When the Mets were finally back in the World Series in 1986, they lost the first two games at home. Then, they got back in the series by taking two out of three up in Boston, and had to take the last two at home. I took the Mason jar, bought an extra lid, put some holes in the top of one, and covered the jar with some waxed paper. Then, I brought it to Game 6. I got there early. From my seat, I could walk down to the right of the dugout. I sprinkled some of the '69 dirt on the field for good luck. And they won that game. Then, I did the same thing in Game 7.

When I first collected the dirt, I had enough to fill about three quart jars, and now I have about one-half of a quart left. I gave some to my brother, Kevin, and I have sprinkled some on the field in front of the dugouts during playoff games. I keep the dirt that I have left in a strongbox because that's how crazy a nut Mets fan I am. I'm afraid somebody will get wind of the fact that I have it and will break into my house and take it. That's the cop in me.

Toward the end of August 2000, my sister Kathy, another big Mets fan, called and asked if I had gotten the _New York Post_ that day. I hadn't, so she told me that Fox Sports Net was running, in conjunction with the _Post_ and the Mets, a "Most Amazing Mets

> **_SPORTS ILLUSTRATED_** was first published in 1954 and its first swimsuit issue was in 1964. The _Sports Illustrated_ Swimsuit Issue has 52 million readers, 16 million of them are females… 12 million more than normal….In 1955, SI selected horse owner, William Woodward, as their Sportsman of the Year. Woodward's wife shot and killed the unfaithful Woodward before the issue went to press. SI then selected World Series hero, Johnny Podres.

Fan" search contest. You were to send in pictures or a video and remarks of twenty-five words or less to enter the contest. I entered and was chosen as one of twenty-five finalists, and then we all had an audition at Shea Stadium. One winner was to be selected and would then be in a Mets commercial. We were told to bring Mets memorabilia, as well as Mets clothing that you'd wear to a game. I had the record album, ticket stubs, articles, and stuff in an album. My brother, Robert, told me to bring my jar of dirt, so I did.

My wife, Joan, and I went down for the audition, and when it was my turn, I put the jar of dirt on the side. I brought the sign I made asking her to marry me and the pictures and ticket stubs from '69 and '73 and a few other items.

When I first sat down, the man holding the audition said, "What's that jar of dirt?" I started to answer him, but he said, "No, no, no, I'll get to that." They asked some questions and had me do some Mets cheers and some other things. When he got to the dirt, I picked it up, and he said, "What's with the dirt?" I said, "This is miracle dust. This is dirt I got after they won Game 5 at Shea Stadium in '69. I jumped on the field and scooped it up into my pockets. It was miracle dirt from the Miracle Mets. It has magical powers." He said, "What are you talking about?" I said, "I used it in '86 when they were in trouble to get them to win." He said, "How do I know that's dirt from there?" I said, "Well, here are the '69 ticket stubs, and here's Game 5." He said, "Oh, wow, really?" I said, "I'm telling you. You can call my friends. This is the real-deal dirt here." He said, "Oh no, we believe you." They took photos of all the contestants, then the audition was over. They told us we would hear from them, and they gave us all some gifts.

After the audition, when the Mets went to the World Series, Adam Miller, a reporter for the *Post*, called Fox to get the name of one of us for a personal-interest-type story. They told him to interview me, saying, "You want to interview this guy. He's got dirt. And he got engaged." So he came out and took pictures of

Joan and me with the dirt and the ticket stubs and the strongbox. I jokingly said, "I guess the secret's out about the dirt now. I'll really have to keep this under lock and key." He said, "Yeah, tomorrow, Tom, the whole world will know about it."

A couple of days later, my brother called and asked me if I had gotten the *New York Post*. I said, "No, but the Mets won so we're one step closer now. There's going to be a Subway Series." He said, "Forget that. You're in the *Post*." I said, "What page, nineteen or twenty?" He said, "You're on page three, almost the whole page."

That was another dream come true. The article talked about both the Mets and Yankees winning. There was a big picture of Joan and me, and it said, "This guy's got all the dirt on the Mets." I saved the paper and we had it open on an easel at our wedding reception.

The guy they ended up picking had a "Mets Room" in his apartment. We saw the commercial once or twice so we figured we were the runner-ups. I wasn't that disappointed because being the nut Mets fan that I am, I thought it was a big honor just to be in the twenty-five. The season ended, then came the Subway Series, which they lost—what could be worse than that? I was on a ledge in Brooklyn for three months! I finally had to get talked inside by the spirit of Gil Hodges!

Then, out of the blue, in March of 2001, spring training camp was getting ready to break, when I got a telephone call from Fox Sports Net. They were calling five of us back—three women, another man, and myself—but not the fellow they chose the year before. They only ran his commercial a couple of times. They asked me, "Would you come in to make a commercial?" I said, "Would I come in—you ain't kidding. Absolutely." They said, "When can you come?" I said, "I'm retired. I can come anytime you want. Is there anything specific I should know?"

They told me to bring the stuff I had brought to the audition the year before. "Make sure you have your Mets stuff on that you wore. Oh, wait a second, there's a note here. You're Tom Flynn, aren't you? Make sure you bring that dirt."

They picked us up in a limo and took us to some place called City Stage in Manhattan. They had scripts for each of us. Mine was written around my engagement to Joan and the dirt. We were there all day shooting the commercials. They did still shots and we did voice-overs, etc. It was fun—a dream come true.

The Mets opened away. The first week I saw one of the women's commercials. Then, one night, we were going out to dinner, and Joan said, "Oh, we've got to tape the game. I don't want to miss it." She went to put the tape in and she said, "Come out here. Your commercial is on." They showed it all year. They also did three billboards with me on them. They used some of our pictures in the *Post* and on ads for Fox Sports Net. I still can't believe it.

Name the
Dodgers manager... win
valuable prizes

HE WAS GOING TO GET TO THE BOTTOM OF THIS EVEN IF HE HAD TO GO ALL THE WAY TO THE TOP

Bill Berensmann

Bill Berensmann, 68, was reared in Brooklyn and is now an architecture professor in upstate New York.

I once sent a letter to Mets president M. Donald Grant. It was the spring of 1977. The Mets were undergoing this massive coup d'etat.

Grant didn't want to pay high salaries, and his refusal was causing all kinds of turmoil. Seaver had told them he wanted a hundred thousand dollars. Grant said, "No way." So I send a letter to Grant because I'm a mad Met fan. I said, "Listen. Give Seaver a hundred thousand dollars. Give Kingman a hundred thousand dollars because he's your best hitter, and then give everybody else on the team ten thousand dollars more. You'll have a happy team. You'll have the best pitcher. You'll have one of the best hitters."

I sent the letter and forgot about it. About three weeks later, it was during spring training, I was at home one night about 7:30 when I got a telephone call. I picked up the phone, and a voice said, "Is this William Berensmann?" I said, "Yeah." He said, "Well, this is M. Donald Grant. I just received a letter from you, and I'd like to talk to you, young man."

My first thought was that this was a friend of mine, but I had never told anybody about writing the letter because it seemed so silly. I wasn't going to go around telling my friends, "Well, I sent a letter to M. Donald Grant." So no one else knew. He was a little bit in his cups. I could tell he'd had a few after dinner or before dinner.

He went into this half hour rambling explanation of why he couldn't do what I suggested: that it would totally upset the budget of the team, that it would spoil some of these guys who shouldn't be getting this much money, that Seaver didn't..." I can't repeat what he said to me. All I can say is that he rambled on for half an hour while I just listened. My responses might have been, "Well, I thought this was a good idea if you pay your best pitcher and your best hitter and keep the team together and don't let it fall apart." He just went on and on and on and on. I was stupefied. I couldn't believe that this man would call me from Florida and take his time to talk to someone who had sent him a letter. I had just said that for four hundred thousand dollars you could have a really happy ball club, and everybody will love you.

Grant was really considered the villain at that time. The team was owned by Joan Payson's family and Grant was the president. Everybody loved Payson because she'd go to the games and sit in her box and wave to the people, but people hated Grant....

When I used to do my yoga, I would chant, "Jerry Koosman. Jerry Koosman. Jerry Koosman." I was a lefty pitcher and Koosman was my idol even though he's probably the same age as me. When he came up, I loved him. He was perfect for yoga. I could really focus on Jerry Koosman.

THEY NAMED BUILDINGS AFTER THIS METS FAN

Bob Brownstone

Bob Brownstone is a high-powered corporate attorney in San Francisco. Raised in Manhattan, Brownstone, 44, brainwashed his daughter. Until she was two and a half, no matter what sport was being aired on television, the toddler would shout gleefully, "It's the Mets! It's the Mets!"

I was starting out as a lawyer in New York City in 1986, and practiced at a fairly big law firm. We were representing Sonny von Bulow through her adult children who were suing Sonny's husband, Claus von Bulow. The only time Claus von Bulow ever testified under oath was in a series of deposition sessions in our office because in his criminal trials he took the Fifth Amendment both times, understandably.

We had about twenty-five attorneys in our litigation group; all of them except two were Mets fans. There were other partners in the firm who had been affiliated with law enforcement, so many of them had blue-collar ties. Even though we were in this corporate environment, people were very down to earth and rooted for the National League.

During the eighth inning of the **HOUSTON** game—Game 6 of the 1986 playoffs—a few of us started infiltrating the conference room, where there was a TV. This was the game that went

On June 15, 1976, the Pirates were "rained in" at the **HOUSTON** Astrodome. Ten inches of rain flooded the Astrodome parking lots and access roads. The teams made it to the park but the umpires, fans, and stadium personnel did not.

sixteen innings. Initially there were only a few of us, figuring, "We'll just watch the last inning and see if the Mets can do anything." The other people in the office were listening on the radio. They knew the Mets were behind and didn't think they had much of a chance.

Around the eighth inning, the Mets were down 3-0, but then they started to rally bit by bit, and more people filtered in. Once the Mets tied it with three in the top of the ninth, more people came in, and as it came to the twelfth and thirteenth innings, pretty soon there were thirty or more people in this tiny room. Whenever there was a key inning, one of the lawyers, David Nathan, got out a pad of Post-its, and said, "Rally Caps." We all put these big yellow Post-its on our heads.

So here we were, these fancy-shmancy corporate litigators sitting with Post-its on our heads, when Sonny von Bulow's daughter poked her head into the conference room, and of course, wondered what we were doing. She later told her friends what a riot she thought that was, all these high-priced lawyers sitting there with Post-its on their heads, watching the playoff game—instead of doing the work they were supposed to be doing....

Oh, the other thing about Game 6—when Claus von Bulow would come to the office for his deposition sessions, he would hang out in the reception area and greet everyone as we came in to work. I presume this was an attempt to charm his opponents' attorneys and their staff. After he was taken to the conference room, he would try to chit-chat with me and the paralegal while we prepared for his deposition. One morning he tried to talk with me about Game 6, saying that he had been at a small dinner party during the game and that baseball's "operative term" seemed to be "first base." How do you respond to that? I couldn't.

IT'S LIKE PLAYIN' HOOKY FROM LIFE

John Camilleri

*John Camilleri is working his dream job. He runs the New York Club-
house Stores of the Yankees and Mets that are owned by sporting
goods tycoon...and nice guy...Jeff Collins. Camilleri, 36, has worked
The Clubhouse Stores for 16 years. Walk into one of the Mets Clubhouse stores and you'll see a sign: "No discount to Yankee fans."*

The Mets Clubhouse Stores are different from any other
sports store. You're walking into a shrine. It's wall-to-
wall Mets. Anything you can think of, anything you can
find, anything in the world with Mets on it we sell—from dog
leashes to women's underwear to men's boxers to the game
on-field jersey on-field jacket. If you want to come in and tell
one of us you want to leave here looking like a Met, we'll make
you look like a Met.

I was a freshman in college and had been a customer at the
store, and I needed a job so came in and filled out an applica-
tion. They liked me, hired me, and I started at $5 an hour in
1990. I've never been on a job interview. I worked as a salesman. I loved sports—loved the business, kept getting promoted
to every level I could possibly go to until where I am now. I
really worked my way up the corporate ladder. I started at the
Yankee stores—in fact I've been traded so many times I feel
like a ball player. I absolutely love it. I always said, "It's never
about the money. The day I wake up and don't want to come to
work, that's the day I start looking for another job." It's like
working for family. It's wonderful!

In 1990, our first store was on 47th Street, Fifth Avenue, right
across the hall from Rusty Staub's restaurant. I started in a
Yankee store, believe it or not. That first store has now moved to

other locations. It was inside a little atrium with no visibility, nothing. We moved to street level—a different world.

What product did we stock that I didn't think would sell well? Easy. That's a 'Mister Met' tee shirt. They flew out of the store. That mascot tee shirt—now you see them on ESPN commercials. We figured it was a novelty. As soon as we got them in, they went right out. It was incredible. We thought the Matsui tee shirts would sell great ... no, not even close. Our best selling item ever has been a Mike Piazza player tee shirt. The day they signed him, they got the best player their franchise has ever seen, without even playing a game. We blew out of his tee shirts. You can't find anything with Piazza on it. We are gonna miss him.

Our Mets and Yankees stores sell game tickets. The first day of new-season ticket sales, we have literally hundreds, if not close to a thousand, of people in line. One year, this one guy had been standing in line for six hours and finally gets up to the window. He asks for four *circus tickets*. He thought we were a place that sells tickets for all events. After I stopped laughing, I had to explain to him in a nice professional way that we only sell Mets tickets. He dropped a few "f" bombs on me. Everyone behind him was shaking their heads. It was in the middle of January so it was pretty cold out, too. Six hours in sub-zero weather...not a very fun day.

We don't sell post-season tickets. We did one year for the Yankees, and it was a nightmare. There were about 2,500 people in line. After the first seven people got tickets, Yankee Stadium was completely sold out so I had to tell about 2,500 people.... After that, I said, "We will never sell playoff tickets—ever, and if we do, I will not be here." They ripped the handles off the door. I had to call the S.W.A.T. team. They closed down Park Avenue and Lexington Avenue, and I needed a police escort home. It wasn't good for business when the newscasters were there. They knew it wasn't our fault...that happened at every other ticket outlet as well.

It's very hard to find good employees. You like to get people who are interested in sports. It's not the same in this day and age. I don't know why that is. I wish I had the answer for that, and, if I did, I'd be a genius. I have no clue why it's hard to find good people. I guess everyone wants to walk in and become C.E.O. entry level. I'm in charge of 13 locations so there are 13 different personalities I have to deal with, as far as managers. I live an hour and a half away from the city, in Holmbrook, Long Island, and I'm never late, never. In the 16 years I've been working here, I have never been late. My philosophy is if you're early, that means you're on time. If you're on time, that means you're late. If you're late, you're fired. That's it. We get kids walking into the store with their hat sideways, pants down to their rear, and dirty sneakers who want to know if we're hiring. "Yeah, we're hiring, but not…." I'll sometimes pull them to the side and say, "You don't come into a job interview looking like this." I guess that's the year 2006—the way kids are these days. Who knows? It's time to change….

Both Mets fans and Yankee fans are very knowledgeable. Both are very passionate. Yankee fans tend to jump on bandwagons whereas Met fans stand proud and true. They both are proud. They both stand by their teams. They're both very knowledgeable sports fans. They both will go through brick walls for a World Series Championship. They're really very similar—there are not many people that really can like them both—it's either/or. That's the way it is. Yankee fans don't like Met fans. Met fans don't like Yankee fans….

A truck accidentally went through the front window of our Met store. It backed up into the front window, and the whole talk was that the "cops were on the lookout for a Yankee fan." It wasn't—it was actually a sanitation truck that went through the front window, accidentally, of course.

IF THE PHONE DOESN'T RING, IT'S RICKEY HENDERSON

Brendan Grady

Brendan Grady works at the New York Stock Exchange and has been a Mets fan most of his 40 years. He loved to call famous sports people in their hotel rooms.

The Mets traded Tom Seaver on June 15 of '77. I didn't go to school on June 16 because I was so upset. I was 11 years old. Seaver was everything. His nickname said it all, "The Franchise." He was the perfect pitcher.

In '97, the Mets played the Orioles in Baltimore on Labor Day weekend. My good friend and I went to Baltimore for the game. We were staying in a hotel across the street from where the Mets were staying in the Inner Harbor. I had a book telling where every major league team stayed on the road. About three o'clock in the morning, we decided we'd make a couple of prank calls and screw around with some of the Mets. We got Bobby Valentine on the phone. He was just making it in from a night game. It happened to be the night that Princess Di died. We told him about it—he hadn't heard word yet. We thought he was going to get off the phone real quick, but he was on the phone with us 40 minutes. We were just going to give him a little s---. We figured he would hang up on us, but he stayed on the phone with us. We had three phones in our room and all three of us were on the phone with him. We talked about everything from that day's game to managing in Japan to a couple of players on the team that he gave us his honest opinion about. It was real neat. The Mets were fighting the Marlins for the wild card that year.

The **MARLINS** went on to win the World Series, the first time they won. He asked if we were coming to the game the next day and we told him, "No, we don't have tickets." He said, "Call me about ten o'clock in the morning, and I'll set it up for you." One of the guys said, "Hey Bobby, we don't want nosebleeds. We want them right by the dugout." He said, "Just call me in the morning. I'll take care of it." We overslept—we were hammered—and we didn't call him.

We were laughing after the call. We got back home on Sunday and called all our friends, telling them we had spoken with Valentine the night after the game. They thought we were kidding and didn't believe us. After Sunday's game, Valentine is talking to a couple of the writers how he had got a phone call in the middle of the night from some guys from New York encouraging him to keep up the fight for the Wild Card. He was talking about us. The Mets were playing the Blue Jays when they got back home from Baltimore. I got some really good seats right next to the Met dugout, and the same four guys went. Valentine is doing an interview with a bunch of reporters behind the cage in batting practice. We yelled out to him, "Bobby, we were the guys on the phone in Baltimore." He shrugged us off, so we repeated part of the stories. He looked over at us and gave us a sign, "Give me two minutes. I'll be right over." He came over and chatted with us. I've met him on the trading floor a couple of times, and he always remembered me.

There were other guys I called, like Chris Sabo, Gary Carter, Thurman Thomas, and Rickey Henderson. I would call the hotel

In the '80s movie, *Back to the Future, Part II*, Biff Tanner scans a sports almanac brought back from the future. Biff reads aloud, "Florida's going to win the World Series in 1997. Yeah, right." The **MARLINS** were not a team at that time, but they did win the World Series in 1997.

and ask for them. If someone is in a hotel, and they don't put the 'do not disturb' sign on, they'll put the call through. I got Sabo a few times, the third baseman for the Reds. I got him when he was getting ready to go to the All-Star Game. David Cone struck his butt out four times in one game at Shea. The fourth time, some fan behind the dugout was giving him some s---, and Sabo started screaming up at him. So, I called Sabo on the phone and said that fan was me. I told him to not make an a-- of himself in the All-Star Game. He told me to go f--- myself. I don't think he meant it in a positive manner.

I used to call Gary Carter all the time. We have the same **BIRTHDAY** so I would call him to say Happy Birthday. I left a message for him when he was with the Dodgers. It was right around opening day. When he got to the hotel and checked his messages, he called me back. I think he was with the Dodgers so that would have been after he had been with the Mets. I had never met him, but he knew I called him every year on our birthday and he remembered my name so he called and wished me happy birthday. I was in my office, and we talked for about five minutes. The people at work didn't believe I was talking to Gary Carter 'cause I didn't answer the call. The person who answered told me I had a call from Gary Carter. When I told her it was *the* Gary Carter, former Met, she was very surprised. It didn't surprise me when he called me back. He's a good guy. He always seemed genuine to me.

> **Frank and Kathie Lee Gifford have the same BIRTHDAY...** they're twenty-three years apart age-wise. They were married in 1986. Frank Gifford was a grandfather at the time. Their children, Cody and Cassidy, are uncle and aunt to Frank Gifford's grandchildren.... When told that Kathie Lee was pregnant, Don Meredith said, "I'll hunt the guy down, Frank, and I'll kill him."

I got Rickey Henderson once. He had run through a stop sign on third base coach, Cookie Rojas, and got thrown out at the plate. He supposedly had a bad hamstring at the time so Rojas put his hands up to stop him as he rounded third, and he ran through the stop sign. I was --------, and I called him up and told him that when the third base coach has his hands up that means 'stop'. He said, "F--- you. If my hamstring wasn't hurt, I would have made it standing up." We talked for about 10 seconds.

I got Thurman Thomas the day after the Super Bowl once. It was the year after he had misplaced his helmet. I told him it was a marked improvement…at least he had his helmet to start the game that year. He thought I was one of his friends playing a prank.

When I would do this at work, I would put the call on a three-way. I would call my friend first and say, "Let's see who we can get now." I had friends listening in to the calls all the time. The last call would have been to Rickey Henderson in '99…

Joe Torre was the worst manager in Met history. Look at his record. Before he got to the Yankees, he was a bad manager. He won once with the Braves. He won his division. He was a disaster in **ST. LOUIS**, and he became a disaster in Atlanta. He was the right guy, at the right time, for the Yankees. The press loves him. Whitey Herzog was the best baseball man who ever worked for the Mets, and the Mets screwed up. They went for the popular choice and hired Yogi Berra as

> **The ST. LOUIS Rams, previously the Los Angeles Rams and before that, the Cleveland Rams, got their nickname from the Fordham football team.**

manager. They should have hired Whitey Herzog. Who knows what the franchise would be today had they hired Whitey?

Davey Johnson was the best manager we had. When they let Davey go, his time had run its course. He had lost control in the clubhouse. Harrelson was a disaster. He was over his head. Some guys weren't meant to be managers. I loved Valentine. He spoke his mind. If something were to go wrong with the Yankees, I think Steinbrenner would look at Valentine very quickly. With Lou Pinella out there, that probably won't happen. I liked Davey Johnson. Davey always swore Whitey was the best. Torbourg was bad. He was the wrong guy at the wrong time. He was just coming off a couple of good years in Chicago. Why did *they* get rid of him—who knows? There had to be a reason. He just wasn't that good. The Marlins proved that out. They fired him in May, hired Jack McKeon and went on to win the World Series...

I'll miss the Bensons—especially her. I'll keep up with her. I think she got her husband traded. She started in on the fact that management just wanted Latin players. I think that's when it was decided that he was out of there...

I feel Shea Stadium is a major s---hole. I'm absolutely in favor of a new ballpark. They should have gotten one before the Yankees. **YANKEE STADIUM** got rebuilt in 1976. They should rebuild Shea right where it is—put it in the parking lot. There is a lot of access. I don't like the way the seats in Shea are. They face straight, especially out at field level. They should be angled toward the field. Shea was built in 1963-64. It's archaic. It was a great football stadium ...

> **The YANKEES once had a bullpen car (Toyota) that fans threw trash at constantly. The trash attracted rats that ate through the engine cables. The car was scrapped in favor of a golf cart.**

The Yankees had **BAT DAY**. When I was a little kid, I thought you were actually getting a major league player's bat so I always wanted my father to take me to Bat Day. He would tell me, "No. You'll understand, when you get older, why we don't go to Bat Day. You don't go to the Bronx when they're giving out bats."

I actually called the Mets to complain about them having Pakistani Night. I told them, "Please tell me this is a ruse—that they were going to have all these people in and were going to bomb them and kill them all and get a new stadium in the process. Please tell me that's what the goal is here." The lady was just dumbfounded that somebody would call up and actually say that.

Orlando Cepeda used more **BATS** than any player in history. He felt each BAT had exactly one hit in it. When Cepeda hit safely, he would discard the bat. He had 2,364 hits in his career.

SO SAY YOU ONE, SO SAY YOU ALL

About a week or so after Bobby V's restaurant in Queens opened, my family decided we would meet there at five o'clock on a Saturday night for dinner. My husband's name is K. C. and we have a Web site, KCMets.com, so we thought we would take some pictures, put together a little story for the Web site, and it would be a nice little adventure.

When we got there, the place was pretty empty. It had just opened, and there hadn't been much publicity about it yet. In fact, Bobby later told us that they wanted to work the bugs out before they had big crowds. So we drove in from our home in central New Jersey with our three kids and a couple of friends, and we wound up being seven people at a table for eight. It turned out that Bobby was in the house. It wasn't very busy and he was very gracious about mingling with all the guests. We asked whether we could ask him some questions.

The benefit of being seven people at a table for eight was that he pulled up the extra chair and really chatted with us for probably twenty or thirty minutes. We talked about his restaurant, his charity work, about how he invented the wrapper sandwich, a whole variety of things.

We would have been so happy if Bobby had just come over, posed for one or two pictures, and said, "Thanks for coming." But he really spent time and talked to us—keep in mind I have three kids, a daughter, twelve, and sons, eight and five, both of whom were wearing their Mets shirts. When he was about to leave, he noticed that my eight-year-old had done a very nice job of coloring his little kids' menu, and he complimented him and gave him a personalized autograph. He even said nice things to my five-year-old, who had only scribbled on his picture, and he autographed that one, too. When he walked away, K. C. said, "That brand of hospitality can't be faked."

———SHARON CHAPMAN, 35, New Jersey

I usually only watch the World Series, and I've only been to two games, but I would love to be married to Bobby Valentine. I like his attitude and I think he's cute. Probably being Italian and around the same age as I am and having a Catholic school background makes me feel like I know him. After all, I would never have known about him if he hadn't been with them. I would never want to break up his marriage, but we all need to dream of something. I'd even go to Japan.

——BARBARA LAROCCO, 55, Queens, Long Island

We were very active in our community and one night we arranged a Family Night. We had about a hundred and fifty tickets, and we all went to Shea Stadium and brought along a gigantic banner. It had to be about forty feet long by four feet high. It was yellow. We opened it up at the seventh inning. It said, "Stem Og Stel." Whoever was broadcasting, it might have been Ralph Kiner, was speculating that we were Swedish. Actually it was "Let's Go Mets" backwards. People finally caught on. When you're looking at it, you can figure it out. That was really a fun night to be there with so many of us there together.

Years later, my son, Jerry, and some of his friends created a banner and went to a Mets game up in Montreal. His mother and I were at home in New York watching the game and lo and behold, we see them on camera walking around the stadium. The banner said, "Allons Mets," which was "Let's Go Mets" in French. We seem to have a knack for getting on television, because the commentators were talking about these guys with the French sign, "Let's Go Mets."

——JOE BROSTEK, 73, New York City, Queens

We had tickets for the first game of the 1998 interleague series at Shea. At the time, we lived up in Ithaca, New York. I had some work to drop off at a Manhattan office, so my wife and I decided to drive down earlier in the day. We found the perfect parking space, right near where we were going, except that we didn't realize that it was a tow-away zone. When we came out, the car had been towed.

We walked up to a police officer who was standing on the corner, and he told us, "Yeah, all the cars get towed from here right at four o'clock." He told us where to go to get the car. This was about 4:30 in the afternoon, and though we had more than enough time to get to Shea for the game, I was beginning to panic. "Oh my God, I'm going to miss the game," I thought. My wife was feeling more like, "Oh my God, We're never going to get our car back."

The impound lot was far from public transportation and it took us a while to get there. When we arrived, one of the cops, noting my Mets-Yankees T-shirt, which I had bought the previous year, asked me if we were going to the game that night.

I looked at my watch and said half-dejectedly that we were going but that we'd probably miss the beginning. I knew that it normally takes more than an hour for a car to be found and processed. Then he asked me which team I was rooting for. I was a little worried what to answer because at the time a lot of people were Yankee fans. This was 1998, and the Yankees had won in 1996, and they were about to win again in `98.

When I pointed to my Mets hat, he jumped up and took the paperwork himself to have the car retrieved. I paid the $45 ticket and $85 for the tow, and we were out of there in about forty-five minutes. We arrived at the game a little after 6:30. By then the place was packed. I think the parking at Shea only holds 20,000 cars, so we had to park out on the grass near the stadium. I kept asking the cop, "Are you sure it's okay to park here? Are you sure I'm not gonna get towed?"

——**ROB STAUFFER**, Formerly of Ithaca, NY

We used to wait overnight to get tickets. I've got my 72-year-old-mom with me, and we get up there, and she wants tickets for a big Sunday game. I told her, "Mom, you've got to come because I can only get eight per person." She's Polish. She comes with me. We're out all night. We were looking at a list of promotion nights. That year, they dropped Italian Night and Polish Night. My father was dying. I said, "Do you believe they dropped Italian Night and Polish Night, and they've got Pakistani Night?" I was ready to walk off the line right there. Those were two of the nights my mom would go to the game. They dropped them both. They had International Week with the Mets—Irish Night, Jewish Night. I came home that night and said, "You're not going to believe this." These are just reasons why I don't care about the Mets anymore. I've been pulling away from the game slowly, slowly, slowly. They know they have you. You're there. They don't care about you anymore.

The worst seats at Shea are obstructed-view seats, which are under the overhang. The Mets sell them as obstructed-view seats for $22. That's the cheapest seat in the house. If you get your hands on them for the Yankees-Mets, it doesn't matter 'cause you're in the ballpark. You're there.

———FRANK CIVITELLO, Brooklyn

Roger Clemens isn't smart enough to know he's dumb

Chapter 4

Playin' Favorites

Put Me In, Coach

HE MIGHT HAVE BEEN SLOW, BUT HE HAD BAD HANDS

Lloyd Flodin

All Mets fans know the players that made it big at Shea Stadium, but what about the thousands of Met farmhands who dreamed of making "The Show" but never did? Lloyd Flodin is a prime example. When Flodin and his best friend, Dennis Wagner, were cut from their New Trier High School baseball team in suburban Chicago, they had limited choices. One was trying to date their prettiest classmate, Ann-Margret (Olsen). They opted instead to go to a gym and lift weights, a practice most coaches forbade at the time.

They continued to lift during their first year at the University of Illinois in Champaign. Then, their miracle occurred. They went out for baseball in college and knocked 'em dead. A year later, Wagner was a Philadelphia Phillies bonus baby, two years later he was in the Phillies big league spring camp with fellow minor league teammates Richie Allen and Ferguson Jenkins. Flodin became captain of the Illini baseball team where one of the pitchers he caught was Jerry Colangelo, who later owned the Phoenix Suns. His summer team's back-up catcher was Jerry Krause, later to find fame with the Chicago Bulls. Flodin, who looked like a California surfer—still does, for that matter—played in the Mets system for six years. When his friend, Duffy Dyer, passed him by, he was traded to the St. Louis Cardinals system. Two years later, he retired and became a professional poker player—decades before it became fashionable.

Walter Milles was the Met scout who signed me. He was scouting me in 1962, right after the Mets were formed. He said, "Would you like to sign with the Mets for five thousand?" After I talked to my college coach and my family, we decided to pass. I went to South Dakota and played in the summer Basin League. Then I played another year for Illinois. Back then, a little over a hundred bucks a week was a good paying job—twenty bucks a day. Five thousand wasn't bad. I wound up signing the next year, 1963. I got seventeen thousand. What they had in those days was a progressive bonus. If you made Double A ball, they give you another thousand. If you made Triple A, they give you another fifteen hundred. Then, if you made the big leagues, they threw in another five thousand. It was a package that was said to be worth twenty-five thousand, but it was seventeen thousand up front.

It was a recruiting process by major league teams because there was no draft—anybody could sign you. I was actively pursued by ten teams. The ones that didn't talk to me knew that they weren't gonna give me any substantial money—Kansas City offered me twelve thousand, The White Sox made me an offer that was low ball. When they did the low offer, I called the Mets and said, "Hey, I'll take it!" It was a neat process. I equated it to getting recruited by a college if you're a high school hot shot in basketball or football. That's basically what it was until the **BASEBALL DRAFT** came in '65, which never affected me. I went to Raleigh, North Carolina, which was the Mets number two farm team. The Mets didn't have a Double A team yet. The Mets had a Triple A team in Buffalo and they had three A-ball teams and Raleigh was their highest one.

Having played in South Dakota for two summers in a strong college league, the Carolina League really wasn't anything other than what I expected. When I got to Raleigh, it was

> **During WWII, the NFL did not refer to the teams' selections of college players as a draft. It was termed the "preferred negotiation list."…BASEBALL DRAFT picks can't be traded for one year. After the third round, there is little difference in quality between start and end of a round…In 1967, the Mets drafted Dan Pastorini, later an NFL star quarterback.**

basically the same thing except the players were a little better and a lot more experienced. In this league, there were plenty of old-timers. We had three or four guys thirty years old on our team. Every team in the league had older guys. Cleon Jones was on the team. Grover Powell was on the team. He was a pitcher who pitched a shutout in his first game in the majors with the Mets. The best player was Grimm Mason but he never made the big leagues. Cleon was good. The guy was big, he was fast, and he could throw. What was confusing to me though, was that the guy was a left-handed thrower and a right-handed hitter. I had only heard of one of those in the whole history of baseball that was a big-league player, Carl Warwick. I was thinking to myself, "Why is he doing this? Why is he not batting left-handed if he throws left-handed? Sort of like Phil Mickelson—why is he a left-handed golfer when he's a right-handed kid in everything he does?" Cleon, you could tell right away, was big-time. In the Mets organization, you didn't have to do much to get well on your way to the big leagues at that point, because they didn't have very many players. We didn't have too many stars back then.

We had a lot of guys that were five and six-year minor leaguers, and they were just playing out the string. Everybody hopes they can make it, but there were not any big stars in the eyes of the older guys who'd been there four or five years. The rookie guys, Wilbur Huckle, Jim Lampe and me, thought we were going to make it.

Swoboda was an amazing guy. He was a hotshot prospect. The Mets were really pushing him hard. He could throw. He could hit. He was a great off-speed hitter and an excellent bunter. We knew that from day one. They couldn't trick him with curve balls and changeups. He only hit about **.260** at Williamsport. One thing about him, when he came into the locker room after a game, he

The difference between a .250 and .300 hitter is one hit per week.

needed his own clubhouse guy. He just took his clothes off, and he hung them right on the floor. If the clubhouse guy didn't hang them up, they never got hung up. He was a nice guy.

At Williamsport in 1965, I thought I was on my way to the big leagues. I was playing great, and then I sprained my ankle. The team went on a road trip. I'm a couple of hundred miles from New York. I said, "Hey, I'm going to New York, just for the heck of it. The World's Fair is going on, and maybe I'll see Shea Stadium." I meet this gal at the Fair who's taking tickets at the AT&T exhibit. She's looking pretty good, and I'm in my twenties. I start talking to her a little bit, and she said she'd get a break in about fifteen-twenty minutes. We walk down into this employees' lounge. There are some people in there, not a lot. I told her I was a ball player in the minor leagues with the Mets in Williamsport, Pennsylvania. There's another guy there about twenty years old. He overhears me. He says, "What's your name?" I said "Lloyd Flodin." He said, "Man, I heard of you in spring training. You hit a home run off Bob Turley, and you were hitting .325. They should have kept you. You're my man. You've got to be up here. We need you. We don't have decent catchers. We need you up here, and we need you now." He's telling me this in front of this gal that I don't even know. I'm going, "This New York stuff is okay. These fans really keep on top of things." The guy knew me from spring training, and I'm thinking I'm just barely a guy out there in the wilderness, so that was neat. That led me to believe that Met fans are like no other fans in the world, and they'd only been in existence for two years.

In 1966, I was back in Williamsport again. We had heard of this phenom, Nolan Ryan at Greenville, South Carolina. We followed the other guys in the minors through the *Sporting News*. Ryan is striking out a bazillion batters in Greenville. By the time the season is over, he had pitched 180 innings and struck out 270 guys. That's thirteen and a half guys a game, and we're wondering! This guy's amazing. Near the end of the year, after his season's over, they call him to Double A, Williamsport. The first game, against Elmira, he had no pitch limit. He pitched ten innings, and he struck out twenty guys. It was the most amazing thing I'd ever seen. He struck out the side in the first inning, and then like two guys every other inning except one, when I think he struck out one guy. He struck out twenty guys in ten innings, and he lost the game 2-1. Davy Nelson, who wound up in the big leagues for six or eight years with Cleveland and Washington, stole home twice. Nolan was new but had a big windup, so he lost that game 2-1. Five days later, they said, "You're pitching five innings, and then five days from now, you're going to pitch in the big leagues." So that game, he pitched five innings, gave up no hits…then five days later he was pitching in the big leagues with the Mets.

He was a great individual with a really neat wife. Over the years, he never changed even with all the success that he's had. He was straightaway, a straight shooter. He was thin. He only weighed about 170 then. He wound up weighing 225 when he finished. It was strictly from working out. This guy was just the straightest arrow you could ever imagine. He had an incredible fastball. He was easy to catch. He had a nice easy motion. People say a fastball rises if it's thrown right. Well, it's not rising. It's just defying gravity more than the other guy's ball. So in relation to other pitchers, it just doesn't get affected by gravity, and people just swing under it. They miss it. He didn't really have much control at that point on his curve ball, but he did have control on his fastball. That game when he struck out twenty, I don't think he walked more than two guys. 'Cause if you pitched ten innings and walk a lot and striking them out, you would have thrown 200 pitches. I tell you his pitch count at full game was maybe 140, 145. They didn't have pitch counts then. In reality they could have, obviously, but they never did, and it didn't seem to affect anything. Pitch counts didn't get important until **BILLY MARTIN** went to Oakland and pitched those young guys all the time.

My favorite story in that regard is in 1974. Nolan, of the California Angels, hooked up in a pitching duel with Luis Tiant of the Red Sox. The game went 15 innings. Tiant pitched 14 of them. Nolan Ryan pitched all 15 innings. He threw a total of 235 pitches that day. Of course, that ruined his career…because 19 years later, he had to retire!

When you're in the minors, you do follow the guys in the big league very, very closely, particularly the guys in your position. That's what you're aiming at. Jesse Gonder is up there, and Jerry Grote and Choo-Choo Coleman—you don't follow the older guys as much because you know they're gonna peter out, like J. C. Martin. He was just hanging on. You definitely follow them. It's like the Vice President who's only a heartbeat away from being the President. It's the same thing. If you're going good, and the guy up there gets hurt, boom, you can be up there in a heartbeat.

When I was at Triple-A Jacksonville, Swoboda was back in the big leagues. Tug was there. Kevin Collins was there. Koosman was there. Koosman was quiet, real quiet. He was a guy who wasn't highly thought of when he first signed. He snuck up on the Mets. As good as he became, they had no reason to think he was going to be that good. There was a funny story about his signing. An usher at Shea had a son in the military down in Texas. Koosman was pitching for the military team. They had a Mets scout, Red Murff, go look at him. They just said, "Okay, as a favor to this Shea usher, or because the guy is left handed,

> When the George Brett "Pine Tar" game was concluded, Ron Guidry was the center fielder and Don Mattingly was the second baseman and **BILLY MARTIN** read the comic pages in his office.

we'll sign him." So Koosman was just going through the minor league system slowly without much fanfare, not thought of any more highly than anyone else. Then, all of a sudden, he had a good year in Triple A, and he's in the Bigs.

Whitey Herzog was never a manager in the Mets system. He was the Mets farm director. He was the best. He had a bigger impact on more players than anybody in the Met system. He gave you the straight scoop. Whitey was amazing. Most general managers, or farm directors, or whatever, wouldn't level with you. One thing he did was amazing; when you left spring training—there were a lot of married guys in the minors—maybe ten guys on the team, and what would happen is some of these farm directors would say, "We're all flying together. We're flying as a team." So from Florida up to Williamsport to start the season, the wives had to drive their cars full of stuff, and some of them even had kids. It was just brutal. Whitey said, "No, don't worry about it. Just take your time, and drive your wife and family and get there in a couple of days." Whitey had real empathy for the players. You could just tell that he was really a people person. Whitey was great. Whitey was smart and a great judge of talent. He really got upset when they thought about trading Nolan Ryan. Then, he went through the roof when Amos Otis was traded to Kansas City for Joe Foy.

I am a die-hard Mets fan. They signed me. They owned me basically for six and a half, seven years. I am a Met fan to this day. I wouldn't trade my Mets for anything. I didn't make much money. I just made enough to eke out an existence, although the bonus certainly helped. It was fun.

TOM SEAVER WAS JUST A REGULAR GUY WHO SOME DAYS WORE A CAPE

Martha Lorenz

Lifelong Mets fan, Martha Lorenz, 44, grew up in Connecticut and now lives in Tallahassee, Florida, where she conducts research and development for a closed-captioning company. She may not go down in history books alongside "Casey at the Bat" poet Ernest Thayer, but her paean to Tom Seaver preserves memories of just how angry the Mets once made her.

My grandmother, who lived in Greenwich, Connecticut, was a Mets fan. Actually, she was a Willie Mays-Duke Snider fan. When the Brooklyn Dodgers and New York Giants left New York, she was one of those people who was never going to root for the Yankees, so then the Mets came along, and she was just a Mets fan from the beginning.

Tom Seaver was my all-time favorite. It was easy to root for him. As a kid, I knew his real name was George Thomas Seaver and that he had a dog named Slider. It was a black Lab. I was never one to write letters or lean over the railing to get autographs. I was just a passionate, live-and-die fan. It would practically make me cry when Seaver would get pounded, which luckily did not happen very often. He always came so close to throwing no-hitters, and then finally he did it when he was on the Reds. Some people like players who are more flamboyant, but Tom Seaver just seemed to take a lot of pride in going out there every fourth day—and back then pitchers used to actually throw complete games.

When Seaver had his back trouble, I remember reading an article in **SPORTS ILLUSTRATED** magazine that talked about

When *SPORTS ILLUSTRATED* celebrated its 50th anniversary, the magazine still had 8,330 of its charter subscribers.

how he had had the slightest change in his motion because he was favoring one leg muscle. It really aggravated the injury in his back. He and Jim Palmer were two of the pitchers of their time who were cited as being the most mechanically correct pitchers. Palmer had much more of the fluid graceful motion, and Seaver really drove with his leg low to the ground. It was amazing that he had such great control and velocity with such power from his legs. He had a great bearing about him when he pitched and never seemed like some overblown caricature of a ball player.

When the Mets traded Seaver away the first time in 1977, I was appalled and disheartened. His press conference was sad. He didn't want to leave. The Mets management decided that he was not worth what he was asking. I guess one could have made an argument in that regard because he had back trouble and they really didn't know how much more of a career he was going to have. But it almost seemed like the team owed it to him after all he'd done. For a long time, he was the only one who put fans in the seats. The Mets were really terrible for a while. Even when he wasn't exceptional, he always managed to do pretty well. It's hard to win a lot of games on a team that just doesn't win much. He was the one performer that everybody hung their hats on and really enjoyed going out to watch. It was hard for a while to take any pride in being a Mets fan, but you could always take pride in being a Tom Seaver fan.

I was at my dad's house in Westport, Connecticut, when I composed the poem. I was twenty-two years old and was a student at Kenyon College in Ohio. It was early 1984, shortly after Tom Seaver had been signed by the Chicago White Sox. I was disgusted that the Mets had let Tom Seaver get away again. They had raised everybody's hopes when they got him back for the 1983 season. He was back where he was supposed to be. He should never have played for anybody else to begin with. It felt like he ended up playing more games for other teams than he played for the Mets in his career. I was just sitting there and talking about the situation, and the words all came into my head in a rush. After I wrote the poem, I probably just put it away in a drawer.

It was nice to be able to put thoughts on paper when I wrote the poem, but it wasn't cathartic. I felt like I was stealing because I was using Ernest Thayer's verse from "Casey at the Bat," and thinking in my own words. I was disgusted with Mets management. I had no idea what they thought they were doing. They had no clue about putting a team on the field that the fans would respond to.

After Seaver retired, my grandparents got me his autograph on a birthday card. Seaver lived in the same town, Greenwich, and my grandfather volunteered at the local YMCA, where Seaver visited and gave some talks. They were so excited, but I couldn't even read the card because I was too nervous.

Name 3 things that will
soften your brain:
Rootin' for the Knicks
Rootin' for the Yankees
And a crowbar

Tom Seaver
A Mets fan laments the loss

(Adapted, loosely—and with apologies—
from Ernest L. Thayer's "Casey at the Bat")

The feeling was betrayal for the Shea faithful that day,
For M. Donald Grant had Tom Terrific traded away.
While the Mets had mainly lost, Tom had always won and won;
He asked from them what he was worth, and so then he was gone.

A straggling few still went to Shea, in deep despair. The rest
Clung to that hope which springs eternal in the human breast:
They thought, "If we'd be rid of Grant and McDonald, the hack,
We'd put up even money that we could get Seaver back."
But Grant and McDonald stayed; nary a good trade they'd make
For the former was a turkey, and the latter was a flake.

Upon the stricken multitude grim melancholy stayed
As there seemed little chance of Seaver coming back to Shea.
Then Grant and McDonald did leave, and in came Doubleday
He brought Cashen, who promised a team that really could play;
And when the dust had lifted, and the fans saw what had occurred,
There was Rusty Staub pinch-hitting and Foster batting third.

Then from a million throats and more there rose a lusty scream;
It rumbled all through Forest Hills, it rattled around Queens;
It pounded in Flushing Meadow and recoiled off the beams;
For they'd brought back Tom Terrific, the answer to our dreams.

There had been a tear in Seaver's eye when he'd left this place
Now there was a pride in Seaver's bearing, and a smile lit his face;
He walked in from the bullpen, and we all knew it was a fact –
It was Opening Day, and yes, we'd gotten Seaver back!

A hundred thousand eyes watched him as he kicked away dirt;
Fifty thousand tongues applauded when he tugged his shirt.
Then while the waiting hitter adjusted bat, foot, and hip,
Adrenaline pumped through Tom; his arm came hurtling through the air,
And Pete Rose could only stand and watch in amazement there.
At the knees a '69 fastball by him quickly sped—
"I never did see it!" cried Rose. "Strike one!" the umpire said.

From the bleachers, packed with people, there came a thund'rous roar:
"Now the magic is back!" they screamed. "It's like it was before!"
And then there were two strikes; Tom took a breath and reloaded
And soon as Rose had fanned, Shea Stadium exploded.

With grim determination the great Seaver's visage shone;
He stirred the fans still further as the tight contest wore on.
He nodded to the catcher, and strike upon he threw
He blew away the Phillies—Rose, Perez, and Mike Schmidt, too.

"Terrific!" fans shouted, and came their echo: "Terrific!"
But throughout the season, Tom's team was (again) horrific.
From April 'til July, few Mets scored but Tom pitched fine;
Then he slipped a bit, and his total wins were only nine.

But the fans came back in droves—they were pleased, and so was Tom;
It seemed the ownership wanted to bring a pennant home.
Surely Doubleday and Cashen knew fans adored Seaver's craft...
Then came January, and once again the Mets gave him a shaft.

When we dared hope incompetence was gone from the front office,
Some imbecilic fool left Seaver off the "Protected" list.
And Shea Stadium now a heart, a soul, and fans shall lack
For this time, we won't be able to get Tom Seaver back.

———**MARTHA G. LORENZ**, February 4, 1984

ROOTIN' FOR THE METS WAS LIKE FLYIN' TWA FOR THE FOOD

Jim Baker

Jim Baker, 45, grew up in Jersey idolizing Jerry Grote. He lost his Mets intensity while a student at Rutgers, but since has regained it in spades.

I played **LITTLE LEAGUE** baseball, and I remember briefly wanting to be Jerry Grote. Grote was my favorite player. The difference between being a kid now and being a kid back then is that there weren't many souvenirs available. You might go to the stadium and get a hat on hat day. Or you might be able to buy a hat somewhere if you looked around, but there weren't any T-shirts. You could not get replica jerseys. I remember I traded a guy some G.I. Joe stuff and he stenciled for me a plain, white T-shirt with Jerry Grote's number and his name on the back. I wore that shirt around the neighborhood every day.

I emulated catchers. I was a heavy kid, and coaches always stuck the heavy kid behind the plate. I was the catcher, and I loved catchers' mitts. I loved the way Grote threw the ball back to the pitcher. He snapped his wrist and threw it back faster than it came in. He had a real gun for an arm. Another thing about coming of age as a baseball fan in that period was that your concept of what numbers were was really skewed, because back then there wasn't a lot of talk about ball park statistics. Grote didn't have outrageous stats—none of the Mets did—because Shea was a pitchers' park. Carl Yastrzemski led the American

> Carl Yastrzemski, from Bridgehampton, Long Island was the first **LITTLE LEAGUER** to be elected to the Hall of Fame. Yaz signed with the Red Sox during his sophomore year at Notre Dame.

League in 1967 with a batting average of .301. I focused more on Grote's defense than his offense. I also liked his intensity.

My friend, Dave, and I had a league we invented. We would play pantomime games. We'd create games with fictitious players, but sometimes we had parody names of real players, like Rusty Slob instead of Staub. We'd steal names from *MAD Magazine*. It got real elaborate. We were playing a 108-game schedule for a while. How much of that had to do with the Mets, I don't know. Sometimes we'd have the actual Mets playing an exhibition game against one of our teams from our invented league, just to amuse ourselves.

Tom Seaver was a favorite of mine. I really grew to like him in the last years of his career, in the 1980s. I remember seeing him pitch against Kansas City when he was with the White Sox. I had great seats for that game, and felt nostalgic that he hadn't lost his ability. He pitched a fantastic game. I stood and applauded as he walked off the field.

I also saw Seaver's 300th victory at Yankee Stadium. Going into Yankee Stadium and being able to root—and I always root against the Yankees, they're evil on earth—was a real thrill for me. Tom Seaver provided a lot of continuity in my life. The second time I cried over baseball was when he got traded to the Reds. I just thought that was the worst. If I weren't a loyal person by nature, I probably would have turned on the Mets for good that day.

The Mets, to me, represent the ups and downs of life because they are a very cyclical team. When they bottom out, they bottom out bad. When they win, they win in a fashion more exciting than any other team. There are real highs and lows. I don't think there's any team that does highs and lows the way the Mets have done in their history. Many teams that never win don't have the highs. The Yankees don't have the lows. Shea Stadium is a very depressing place when the Mets are down. It feels like Siberia—there's a "win" chill factor. You could probably say that about a lot of places, but when you've been there at its height, and then you've also been there at the bottom, there's a great incongruity there. I've gone through most of my life not really expecting that much from the Mets. The first two years I rooted for them, 1967 and 1968, they were wretched. They were really bad in '68. I grew to expect it. To see them was enough.

The Mets let Nolan Ryan get away, too. Personally, I never had a problem with the Mets trading him. But I did have a problem with who they got for him—Jim Fregosi. They had to give up three other players, as well. Leroy Stanton was the best of the other three. In the late 1970s, he had brief success with the Mariners. I distinctly remember going to a game in '71, Ryan's last year with the Mets. It was against the Phillies. Ryan **WALKED** the first three batters he faced. Then, he struck out the side so he got out of the inning with no runs, but it was nerve-wracking. The Mets just couldn't handle the walks anymore. They had a surplus of arms. Fregosi was a total bum, just a stiff. He was done by then. He had a fairly good run in the sixties, but by the time the Mets got him, he had nothing left in the tank.

I was at Shea one night in the 1980s, and Keith Hernandez would not run ground balls out. He hit a hard grounder and walked to first base, and there was a double play. I stood up and I yelled, "Hernandez, why don't you hustle?" I thought I was gonna get lynched. People loved him so much they were willing to overlook that. There were a lot of things about him I liked. He's one of those people who's too complicated to dismiss with one sentence. One thing that always blew my mind about him is that he was well known as a Civil War buff—and as a former cocaine user! I'm thinking, "You're sitting there reading Bruce Catton and snorting cocaine!" But I loved his plate discipline. I loved his defense. I liked his game.

> **Between WALKS and strikeouts, Mickey Mantle went the equivalent of seven full seasons without putting the bat on the ball.**

DWIGHT GOODEN:
THE PROMISE OF A LOVER,
THE PERFORMANCE OF A HUSBAND

Charles Levine

Charles Levine, 44, is a financial advisor in the Twin Cities. He moved to Minneapolis from Brooklyn.

It was a lot of fun to go to Mets games in the eighties when Doc Gooden was on fire. You were rooting for his strikeouts, rooting for him to break all sorts of records. I was even rooting for him to break Seaver's records. To me, records are okay if they're broken by the right guy, and the right guy is the guy on your team.

Gooden wasted a good career. He wasted a great career. I apparently have very little room in my pantheon for him for doing that. After two seasons, at the age of nineteen, he had over forty wins, had an incredible ERA, had all these strikeouts, had potential. My friends and I were talking about him winning four hundred games, not three hundred. After that second season, I talked to one of my friends and told him that the Mets should trade Gooden now. His trade value would never get higher and most pitchers don't sustain that kind of performance. Every now and then you find a **ROGER CLEMENS** or a Tom Seaver who fifteen years later is still doing it, but most pitchers don't. My friend said I was nuts. Not too many years later, he said, "You know you were right. I always remember you said that, and by God, you had it right." Gooden threw with his right hand, drank with his left hand and threw his career away with both hands.

> In 2001, **ROGER CLEMENS** won his sixth Cy Young Award even though he did not throw a complete game that season.

In my teens, I used to like to figure out Tom Seaver's ERA, batter by batter in my head. I'd be sitting in Shea Stadium with my friends. It'd be the middle of the season. He'd have 150 innings and his ERA going into the game was 2.48. It would be even better when his ERA was like 2.51 so he was looking for that milestone. What would it take for him to get that ERA under 2.50? Going into the game, I'd be thinking, "If he pitches eight innings with two or fewer runs, or seven innings with one or fewer," and I would calculate roughly where his ERA was gonna be. "Okay, he went through another inning—okay, that's a ninth of a game, do that math and just figure out where his ERA is." I wanted to know what was going on and how well he was doing. I just wanted that proof that he was the best. Some people were swayed by the fact that Seaver was a blabbermouth and had an ego that wasn't small, but I didn't care.

I remember the story that he apparently lost the 1971 Cy Young award because he had bragged to the press that he presumed he would win it because he had a better winning percentage than Fergie Jenkins who also won twenty games, although Fergie had more wins.

The day the Mets traded Tom Seaver was the worst day of my youth. Who they got (Pat Zachry, Doug Flynn, Steven Henderson, Dan Norman) seemed good at the time, but it wasn't the right thing to do. They traded the franchise and they had no right to do that. I certainly hated the Mets at the time, but there weren't really any alternatives. As a proper Mets fan, there's no way you're gonna root for the Yankees. You just won't do that. Nothing else made sense.

BITS AND BITES, BEGGED, BORROWED AND STOLEN

When I was a kid, Tom Seaver was a god to me. I saw National League teams all the time because I was a Mets fan. Willie Mays, Sandy Koufax, Bob Gibson, these people were literally, literally gods to me. To this day, I don't really care to find out that "so and so" wasn't a good guy. That doesn't matter to me. It's like watching an old-timers' game, and seeing some guy who has a gut that comes out six feet past his belt line. I don't need that as a memory. I don't need to wait on line for two hours to spend a hundred dollars for an autograph.

Autographs never interested me. I have a kind of "mental museum." I can just go back in my mind and say, "That day up in Boston was like a Monet. It looks better and better from a distance." Which is exactly what an impressionist painting looks better from—a distance. I have this wonderful group of memories associated with being a Mets fan and with baseball. It's like a golden string that attaches through my whole life. It's probably the only constant that I've had since I was a child up to this moment.

———PATRICK HOGAN, 47, Brooklyn

I went to one spring training game as a kid, in St. Petersburg, Florida. After the game, the players left Al Lang Field in their uniforms and were waiting at the curb for cabs. I took this opportunity to ask for autographs. This was when I turned to Jerry Grote. I went up to him and said, "Could I have your autograph?" He said, "Look out behind you, there's a cab coming." I turned around, and there was no cab, and he moved away. If Jerry had known that I was in Florida because my grandmother had died....

The guy who stayed behind and signed autographs after all the other players left was Tug McGraw. Years later, he spoke at one of my Little League banquets and was very funny. He made a Sammy Davis, Jr., joke, which was probably written for him. It didn't go over very well. It was the year after the Mets had won it all so he was probably busy on the banquet circuit and probably had a lot of prepared material.

"Those kids from the Piscataway Little League are going to love this 'rat pack' material that I've prepared," he told the audience. He was late, too, and they called a local guy, Jeff Torborg, to warm up everybody until McGraw arrived.

———**JIM BAKER**, 45, New Jersey

The first time I went to Shea Stadium, I was just overwhelmed. I wasn't expecting to be there. I thought the whole thing was overwhelming, the city, the fans. The first time I saw the fans there with their signs and carrying on, I just couldn't get over it. Here in Kansas City, the Royals didn't have fans like that.

I lived in a hotel out by LaGuardia Airport. A lot of other players lived there, too, Galen Cisco—the former **OHIO STATE** fullback, Carlton Willey, Tug, Swoboda. We didn't even have a car. If we'd go downtown, we'd take the subway downtown to Manhattan on days off to do things down there. The hotel had a shuttle to take us to the ballpark. Larry Miller was the only player I remember having a car there. When he came inside to check in, somebody robbed him before he ever got back to his car— cleaned him out. Sometimes, fans would be there in the hotel. They'd be coming up to get autographs or to talk to us. It's hard to remember thirty-five years ago.

In the 1976 **OHIO STATE**-Indiana game, the Hoosiers scored first. Indiana coach, Lee Corso, called a timeout. During the timeout, Corso had his team pose for a group picture with the scoreboard—showing Indiana leading Ohio State 7-0—clearly visible in the background. Corso featured the picture on the cover of the 1977 Indiana recruiting brochure. Ohio State won the game 47-7.

After the World Series in '69—the Miracle Mets—I was living in Memphis and working for a glass company in the off-season. Swoboda came down to speak at some sports banquet they were having. I met Swoboda at the Peabody Hotel, and we were sitting there waiting for the ducks. Jack Buck comes walking by and says, "Hi Ron, how you doing? Hi, Jim." It just shocked me that he remembered who I was—four years later. I was impressed 'cause I was just a one-year deal in New York, and he was in town for this banquet. The fact that he knew who I was was pretty impressive to me. He just had that kind of a memory.

Buck was the master of ceremonies and Swoboda was one of the main speakers. He had been brought in to speak because the Mets had just won the World Series that year. Swoboda was having contract negotiation troubles. He was holding out. He spent the whole weekend calling them and negotiating—no agents back then.

——JIM BETHKE, Los Angeles; Kansas City native, 2-0 in his only year with the Mets in 1965.

I never got into any of the good seats, mostly the cheap seats, but I was just totally mesmerized by the aura of the field and the history behind some of the ballparks. My uncle would drive me down to the Grand Central Parkway, leaving Shea Stadium. I remember looking out the rear window and I would say to myself, "I'm going to be there one day. I'm gonna play in that stadium one day"…and it came true for me.

——WILLIE RANDOLPH, Yankee star, Mets manager

First stadium I ever saw: Shea Stadium…it just seemed so enormous to me. I knew that this is the big leagues, this is what it's all about, what you work for all your life. But I think that the size of the stadium, the fact that people are actually coming out,

WILLIE RANDOLPH'S brother was drafted by the Green Bay Packers and played for the New York Jets.

paying to watch you play, is what you think about. And the excitement of it is a great thing.

———**MO VAUGHN**, ex-Met

My dreams about becoming a Major League Baseball player... came true in New York. When I walked onto Shea Stadium in my Mets uniform for the first time, I felt like I was the luckiest guy in the world because every day when I came to work for the Mets, I would go to Shea Stadium, play big-league baseball. And then, after the game, walk across the street and go to the World's Fair. It was just too good to be true.

———**TUG McGRAW**, 2001

The first time when I went to Shea Stadium to see the Mets, I was in the nosebleed seats way up there. They used to hit pop-ups and you think it's coming to you, and the ball wouldn't be close to me—it'd be either on the field or in the first section. And I just remember always wanting to get a ball. And I felt like all the players heard me and knew that I was up there cheering for them. And that was a thrill.

———**ERIC YOUNG**, later a Major Leaguer

In 1964, my family and I traveled to New York City for the World's Fair. The Fair was across from the ballpark. We wandered over to Shea Stadium. It happened to be open, so we walked in. As a freshman in high school, my dream was to play professional baseball. As I stood at home plate, the stands towered above like nothing this small East Tennessee country boy had ever seen. I told my mom and dad, "Someday, I'll play here." My first year in the big leagues was with the Oakland A's; we played in Shea because Yankee Stadium was being renovated. Dreams do come true.

———**PHIL GARNER**, Major League player and manager

The most pronounced fan at Shea Stadium when I was there who is in all the Mets highlight films over the years is a guy named Karl Ehrhardt. He was a sign-maker. That was his business, I believe; although, I never really met the guy. You were constantly aware of him because he would react to things on the field with perfectly timed signs. He'd have names for players. In fact, I remember seeing a sign after my catch in game four of the World Series, he puts up, 'Fan-tas-tic.' That was what was cut into the footage I saw. It was incredible. He had this big portfolio of signs, and he'd take them out and unfold them. I guess he had a little code there that told him what the sign was and what he had for that particular day. He'd break out a new one every once in a while but he had his perennials. He wasn't a big fan of Ed Kranepool. He called him 'Super Stiff.' Eddie didn't warm to that very well, and I don't blame him. He was very inventive, and he was a huge part of the game because he was right behind the dugout. When something would happen, everybody would look to him to give it its official response. I thought he had died, but somebody told me he was still alive. I've never been in any ballpark in the major leagues where anybody was as good as he was. He was laser-sharp. He was right there. He was right on it. His timing was incredible.

The Yankees never had anything like that. They didn't allow signs. You had signs all over the ballpark. Sign Day was great. Banner Day—nobody else had that. Banner Day is on a couple of those Met highlight films, and it's incredible. I remember my number was four, and someone had a sign saying, "I'm such a big fan of Ron Swoboda, I had four kids."

There was a guy named Dr. Principato. He was a radiologist who ran around in a yellow poncho with 'Go Mets' on it. He was behind the dugouts, up the aisles, all over the place, exhorting fans. I've said 'Hi' to him a couple of times along the way and always appreciated him. He's a cheerleader. He's like these guys that are just so completely absorbed by the fact that they're in a ballpark that they want to fire people up and create the same excitement that's going on inside of them.

Are they normal people? Probably not. It's one of the manifestations of 'crowd,' I guess is the best way to put it, without having any degree in psychology. They embellish the experience inside a ballpark. We were aware of them out on the field. I always looked—hell, my head was in the stands half the time anyway. I always wanted to see what was going on.

Wilbur Huckle, I'd love to know where Wilbur Huckle is. He was from Texas and played in the Mets minor-league system. He had those big hands, probably Germanic. I remember kicking back before the games, players want to rest before the game, they don't want to wear themselves out. Huckle would run about five of the hardest sprints that you could ever imagine. The manager would ask him, "What are you doing?" He said, "It's an adrenalin run. I'm trying to build up my adrenalin." Huckle was great.

What incredible, wonderful, wonderful memories I have of Shea Stadium and those great Met fans.

——**RON SWOBODA**, Mets outfielder, 1965-'70;
now a sportscaster in New Orleans

The first time I saw Shea Stadium, I was so impressed with how big it was, just huge. I also remember all those jets flying over all the time. You couldn't hear anything. You couldn't even hear yourself talking it was so loud when they were over the stadium. You go back that far and it's just like a dream.

I made the club in spring training when Art Shamsky got hurt. I started as right fielder in New York. Hodges and the others didn't know who I was at first....1969 was my first year on a major league contract. They took me on a road trip, which they hadn't planned on me going—except Art hurt his back. They started me, and I went on a thirteen-game hitting streak, and they were forced to keep me.

When I first got there, I stayed in Manhattan as Kenny Boswell's roommate. That lasted about a month. Then I lived in Flushing and Forest Hills and Queens. I was everywhere. I was single.

The Met fans are the best. I still love going back to New York and seeing those people. They're amazing. I had fans call me recently from New York and they go on and on and on. They know more about the game and statistics than you and I do. They're amazing people. I really enjoy going back there. They're really fans. I still get some mail from fans. There's not any particular fan over the years that I've been in regular contact with. Just going back for card shows and seeing people waiting in line. They treat you like you're something really special. 'Course I don't think I'm that special—we're all the same. I can remember people waiting in line for card shows and they're shaking. I guess they think about that year and that team, and they're shaking when they meet you. It's just unbelievable how they are. They just love the game so much. If I had the option to play anywhere, I'd play right there in New York—no doubt.

My wife and I went to a game the other night in the Angels' Stadium, which we very seldom do. That stadium was so quiet. It was just quiet in there. But New York...I just get fired up thinking about them right now, they know the game. They love you, and they hate you, and there's no BS with them. They lay it out on the line to you. I like that.

——**ROD GASPAR**, Mets outfielder, 1969-'70

My friends and I were so consumed with the Mets that my reputation was well known in school. I had one of those zip-around autograph books and one of the guys wrote me a poem:

Here comes Tug, ready to relieve
I'm a Met fan, ready to believe

Then he signed it, "Nice knowing you. Good luck. Let's go Mets."

Years later, when I was in my early twenties—well past the 1973 Mets—I had a friend who worked as a cocktail waitress in a lounge not far from LaGuardia Airport and Shea Stadium.

She would say, "Oh, some of the Mets came in." And she would tell me stories about talking to the players. It was hard for me to believe the Mets would be doing the things she described, because they were always so perfect in my mind. I couldn't believe they would go to cocktail lounges, hang out, drink, and carouse. I always had this puritanical picture of them because I was thirteen when I began to like them so much. It was hard for me to discover that even heroes had feet of clay.

——ANDREA MALLIS, 45, Flushing native

There's only one autograph that was special to me and I got it at spring training. It was Tom Seaver's. I had him write it to my father.

It was 1999, the year he was at spring training helping out the pitching staff. He was just walking down Willie Mays Lane all by himself. When he was about twenty feet away, I said, "Excuse me, can I ask you for an autograph?" He walked toward me and said, "Well, you can ask, but that doesn't mean I'm going to give it to you."

I continued walking and he put his arm over my shoulder, and we continued walking the length of the field. There were a bunch of fans, and I said to him—I got a little nervous—"I was really young when you pitched so I don't really remember, but my dad's always told me this and such and such." As people started to come over, he told them, "Leave me alone, I'm talking to my daughter now."

I don't remember very much about it. He may have needed someone to protect him from the crowd—but he chose me! He could have just picked a colleague and said, "We're working now." But I thought that was really great. I said, "My dad told me there was a game you pitched and there was a pitch you knew you were gonna need to get someone out, and you didn't use it until late in the game. I don't remember who it was." He answered, "That was Dave Winfield."

I don't know if he was talking about the same thing that I was. That was Tom Seaver. This wasn't even my idol, this was my dad's favorite player.

We walked the full length of this field. I was really nervous and excited. I had a book I had brought, and I said, "It's for Seymour." He started to write, and I spelled out, "S-E-Y-M-O-U-R". He said, "I know. I can spell. I went to college." He wrote, "My very best wishes to Seymour, Tom Seaver, Number 41." He gave it to me and walked away.

Then, all the crowd came over to me. They were like, "Oh wow, what'd you get?" "I got an autograph for my dad," I said. Then a guy came over, a random guy, and he said, "I took a picture of you while you were walking. If you give me your address, I'll mail it to you." So, I gave this stranger my business card, and when I got home, I got the photograph in the mail. I put it in a frame with the autograph and my ticket stub for the day. Then, I gave it to my dad.

Dad loved it! The first thing he did as he looked at it he said, "He's really listening to you. You're obviously talking in the picture. That means he's a good father to his children." My dad displays it at home, not only because I gave it to him, but, if I can speak for my dad, I think it signifies to him my daring and boldness, that I am able to go out and do that.

——RACHEL EISENMANN

In 1974, there was an accident at a plant I owned in the Quad Cities, and a young man got burned very badly. His favorite player was Nolan Ryan. The California Angels were scheduled to play an exhibition game against their Quad City Midwest League team one night in August. I called the visitors' locker room in Kansas City where the Angels were playing. I asked Nolan—if I picked him up at his hotel in the Quad Cities, would he go visit this kid in the hospital. I told him I'd pay him what-ever it would take. Ryan said, "That's ridiculous. I'll be glad to go see him, but I'm not going to take any money for it." The kid was able to get out of the hospital for the exhibition game, and we had seats right behind the dugout. Nolan Ryan said, "As soon as I get done with my workouts, I'll come up and sit with you guys." He did and he brought up an autographed baseball for this young man who had been badly burned. Nolan was terrific and really helped make his painful recovery easier…Ryan would have struck out 7,000 if they hadn't lowered the pitching mound and introduced the DH. For almost all of his career, he played for terrible teams: terrible defensively, weak-hitting, and lousy bullpens. One year, he was 8-16 but led the majors in strikeouts and earned-run average. He lost a bazillion one-run games, or he would have won over 400 games.

Later, Bobby Valentine came up and sat with the young man. We had never met him before. He was great! I knew Valentine was a heavily recruited football player out of Stanford, Connecticut, so most of the time with him was spent talking about football and the different recruiting trips he had been on. He told of how he had been in **JOHN McKAY'S** office at Southern Cal, how he had been in Ara Parsegian's office at Notre Dame, how he'd been in **BEAR BRYANT'S** office, at Alabama. I said, "Well, who offered you the best deal?" He said, "Those three didn't offer me anything. Wake Forest offered me the most." But, he ended up signing a huge bonus baseball contract with the Los Angeles Dodgers.

I was at the game of Nolan Ryan's major league debut in September of 1966 against the Atlanta Braves at Shea. The third batter was Eddie Matthews. After the first pitch, Eddie Matthews stopped, stepped back out of the batter's box, turned to Jerry Grote—we're sitting right behind home plate—and you could "read" what he said to Grote, "What the f--- was that?"

> After the Tampa Bay Buccaneers were trounced by the Giants, a reporter asked Bucs' coach **JOHN MCKAY**, what he thought of his team's execution that day. McKay replied, "That's a good idea" … **BEAR BRYANT** once said, "If I quit coaching, I'd croak in a week." He died 28 days after his final game.

But, Ryan didn't get his first strikeout that night until Pat Jarvis, the Braves pitcher, came up to the plate.

——**DICK FOX**, 64, Falmouth, Massachusetts

I do a lot of freelance editing work for a publisher in New York, and one day I went in to the office wearing all my Mets stuff. A guy said, "Oh, are you going to the game tonight?" So I said, "Yeah, we're hoping to." He said, "Do you have tickets yet?" I said, "No." So he hands me an envelope and as I walk out, I open the envelope, and inside there were two box seats.

So, my wife, Becky, and I go to the game, and we're looking for our seats. We were getting closer and closer to the field. It turns out that back around 1999, two rows were added in the front of the stadium for the playoffs, and that's where our seats were. I've never sat that close. We were ON the field. It was incredible.

The Mets were playing the Orioles. In the first inning, Cal **RIPKEN** comes up to bat, and he hits this little number up the third-base line. Robin Ventura runs in, scoops it up and just fires it over to first. Ripken's out by a mile. He runs past first, makes a turn right in front of us. As he's coming back around— I don't know what seized me, but I yelled practically right in his face, "That's what a real third baseman looks like, Cal."

I don't know where that came from. My wife was completely embarrassed. Ripken went 0-5 for the night. He went on the DL right after that and didn't play the rest of the season.

Becky is still embarrassed about that story.

——**ROB STAUFFER**, Riverdale, NY

I grew up in Port Washington, Long Island, which is the last stop on the Long Island Railroad line that goes to Shea Stadium. In 1985 and 1986, the Mets took over Port Washington,

Doug Harvey umpired over 4,000 consecutive major league games....When Lou Pinella played minor league baseball in Aberdeen, South Dakota, the team's batboy was Cal RIPKEN, Jr.

in a manner of speaking. A lot of the guys hung out at a bar there called Finn MacCools, where they had the party the night they won the 1986 Series. It was a place where a lot of Mets got into trouble partying. Supposedly, **DARRYL STRAWBERRY** would be there 'til all hours, and then be out of the lineup the next day with a "sore back."

Dwight Gooden lived on my block. He lived in a little basement apartment right near the Long Island Railroad stop. I'd see him outside and say, "Hi, have a good game." And he'd say "hi" back. Who knew all the trouble he was getting in to while all of this was going on, but at the time he seemed like a nice enough guy. Even when I was feeling my most lukewarm about the mid-eighties Mets, I always loved Gooden and would root for him like crazy. I would watch whenever he pitched. In 1984, I remember this one-hitter against the Cubs that was extremely exciting. I was always in awe of Bob Gibson's 1968 performance and wondered when a pitcher would come along like that for us. Gooden was like Bob Gibson.

——PETER FORNATALE, 33

The worst Mets player is the guy who manages the Twins now, Ron Gardenhire. When I went to ballgames back in the early 80s, when the Mets were horrible, I couldn't believe he was on the team. One time, he was on third base. They were losing the game 8-0. Someone hits a deep fly ball to center field on the warning track. There's no play at the plate. Gardenhire runs down the line, dives head-first into home plate. He made such an awkward slide that he had to be helped off the field. I would see things like that and think, "How is this guy a major leaguer? How is Ron Gardenhire here? It turns out—he's a great manager. Guys who don't spend too much time playing

> Who is the most famous person to pinch-hit for
> **DARRYL STRAWBERRY**? Homer Simpson, on an
> episode of *The Simpsons*.

make the best managers because they make effort to study the game.

When they traded Seaver, I cried. That was June 15, 1977. That killed me. Back then, $100,000—now they give guys ten million a year. When Gooden came in, now you've got Dwight Gooden—this guy's incredible. I went to the parade in '86 and Gooden's not there. I'm saying to myself, "Where's Gooden? Strawberry's here. How could you miss this parade?" He wasn't there at City Hall. They just shook it off, "He's not here." Then, it was two or three years later when we finally found out the whole bit.

It's scary how good Dwight Gooden could have been. When a pitcher comes up, for the most part, it takes him a few years. Some pitchers don't come into their own till they're 28-29. This kid threw that curve ball—he had everything working for him. He was smart. He knew when and where. It figures he'd turn out to be bad. That's all I would say sometimes. I'm really p------ off at him because he never once said anything. He was always making excuses. Even now, when he gets in trouble, he's always making excuses. It's amazing. Be a man. He was great.

Beltran? Even the Yankees didn't go get him. Cameron, you got a centerfielder. That's the way the Mets do things, again. They gave Cameron away for nothing. Cameron is still a top-notch centerfielder, and there's not too many of them in the league. I just watch the Mets and shake my head. I don't watch as many games anymore. When I was a kid, I would probably watch or listen to every game. I now read about it in the newspaper the next morning. When we were kids, it started at 8:05 p.m. and it was over at 10:10 p.m. every night. It was a two hour and five minute game. Now, the games are over three hours long.

If the Mets had kept Herzog and if Strawberry and Gooden had stayed clean, and if they would have drafted Reggie Jackson instead of Steve Chilcott, who knows? It's that stuff. It's at a different point now where they're 40+ years old. When they were younger, it was okay. Now, they can't play ball with the

Yankees. They can't ever be the Yankees so they don't have to try and do that. They don't have to try and match the Yankees. Just be the Mets. Now, they try to chase the Yankees, and they'll never be that. Part of the reason is that there's more commercial time in between. They want you there longer. They figure if you're there for two hours, you don't have to buy a meal. If they keep you there for three-and-a-half hours, people get hungry, and they spend money. A slice of pizza was twenty cents. The All-Star games were in the afternoons; even the World Series games were in the afternoons…

Back to Clemens. How many games has he pitched now over his career against teams that would never have been a major league team when Seaver was playing? Seaver against Clemens—that's my argument with all my friends. Here's Clemens pitching half the games in his career against minor league teams. I've been telling Yankee fans to look at the size of the guy. He's a friggin' bull. Look at him. No one questions the pitchers about steroids. They're always questioning the hitters. What about the pitchers? Look at Clemens.

If the Mets had kept Herzog and if Strawberry and Gooden had stayed clean, and if they would have drafted Reggie Jackson instead of Steve Chilcott, who knows? We'd no longer be down at the corner of What and If.

——FRANK CIVITELLO, Brooklyn

Chapter 5

On the Road Again

Today We Ride

THE ODDS WERE GOOD...
BUT THE GOODS WERE ODD

Bruce Laxer

A few years ago, Bruce Laxer went to San Francisco—not that there is anything wrong with that. He went there to be a 41-year-old batboy for the Mets. The money manager from Scarsdale had the time of his life.

I was at Game 5 in 1969 when they won it all. I was at Game 7 in 1986 when they won it all. I was a batboy for the Mets five years ago at the age of forty-one. I paid for it at a charity auction, but Bobby Valentine reached into his own pocket to support the charity, the Miami Project, founded by football player Nick Buoniconti.

The way the story was told to me was that Bobby Valentine was at a charity wine- tasting in New York, and he ran into ex-football coach **JERRY GLANVILLE** in the city. Glanville said, "Listen, I'm going to this thing for Nick Buoniconti's foundation. Why don't you come tonight?" That's how Valentine ended up going.

Without prompting, Valentine took the microphone. The Mets had just come off a very good run that year. He started by saying, "Hey, I'm going to have an auction for an autographed ball." That has absolutely no interest for me. You could tell he was well practiced in this technique because when the bidding went dead, he said, "Well, this is not just a regular autographed

> Detroit Tigers manager, Jim Leyland was once a second-string catcher for Perrysburg, Ohio High School. The starting catcher was **JERRY GLANVILLE**.

ball. This is where you come out to the field and you get the autographs of the players."

Well, that's a little bit more interesting, but still not compelling, and the bidding started up again. He said, "And you know, the Mets are really against people coming on the field at Shea Stadium, so how about if we do this at an away game. I'm going to throw in two first-class, round-trip air tickets."

Okay, now you've got my interest because now you're talking vacation. You're talking the whole thing. The bidding continued. Then he said, "You know what, how about if we throw in a uniform." Each break in the bidding, he added something, he kept sweetening the pot. Then he said, "Well, as long as you're with us, you're going to need a place to stay, so two nights at the team hotel." And finally, he said, "And you know what, as long as you're with us—you've got a uniform, you're staying with the team, how about if you're the batboy?"

That was it for me. I bid $4,600. But if that had been a charity auction where they had it preplanned and everybody knew that there was going to be sports memorabilia and sports-related things, that experience would have gone for fifteen to twenty thousand dollars. But people didn't expect that—it wasn't what I had gone for. I snuck away cheap. And then it turned out that while I was doing the batboy gig, one of the regular batboys couldn't show the next day so I ended up with a second day.

It was the best experience of my life. Valentine went out of his way to make it a great experience for me. When I got there, I met him outside. He brings me in—it's about six hours before the game. He saw that I had my glove, and he pointed to center field, as if directing me to go out to center field. I shagged flies with the boys—I mean I was attempting to. I'm in pretty good shape and I'm a good athlete for my age, but I didn't catch anything over my head.

I had never stood so far away from a guy with a bat in his hand. It was like he was in another zip code. I was out there with John Stearns, the former catcher and coach, and he was great. Everybody was just great. I was having the time of my life. Actually during the game, I ran out and got the bats. People were yelling, "Hey, Batman," really giving me a hard time.

None of my friends were there, just my wife and my brother. It was in San Francisco. Don't forget it was an away game. I'm a wine nut so we went to the Napa Valley for a few days. It was just heaven to me. I went out and got the bat each time. I was really involved in the game, just going out there and fielding with the guys. Before I went, I had gone out and bought this little microcassette recorder and a throwaway camera. I had thought, "I've got two young kids." I thought I'd say, "Hey Mike Piazza, do me a favor. Say hello to my son, Jeremy." Or something like that. But once I got there, I said to myself, "You know what, none of that. I'm gonna be the batboy. I'm gonna do what the batboy does." I mixed the **GATORADE**. I picked up the dirty towels off the floor. I cleaned the cleats. I did what the batboys do. I manage money for a living, but I was a child for two days.

Something really special happened before the second game. Bobby Valentine sat down next to me on the bench. He leaned up to me and said, "If so-and-so (the lead-off hitter) gets on, do you think I should hit-and-run with Derek on the first pitch or the second pitch?" You know what I mean, he was just totally trying to goof on me but involve me a little bit. I laughed so hard, I don't think I even answered.

After the first game, I was sitting around with Al Leiter and John Franco. It's unusual for a 40-year-old man to be the batboy

> **GATORADE** is named after the mascot for the University of Florida (The Gators). It was developed by a professor there under a grant from Stokeley-VanCamp.

so they were asking me how I got there. I told them, "Yeah, yesterday's game was great. It was a lot of fun, but my only disappointment was that nobody hit a home run for the Mets." Because if somebody hit a home run, that meant I got to go greet the runner at home plate, pick up the bat, and bring it to the dugout. That would guarantee that my kids would see me on TV.

AL LEITER says, "Hey, you want to guarantee that you're on TV? Tomorrow during the game, why don't you run out and tackle the opposing pitcher? That way you'll be on TV." Of course, he was just kidding around.

For the second game, when the other batboy couldn't come and they asked me to replace him, I asked the clubhouse guy, "Well, how do I get in?" The first time I had walked in with Bobby Valentine—that was no problem. "Just tell them Harvey said it was okay." I looked with a raised eyebrow, but I said, "All right."

So, of course, the second day comes, and I go to the gate. The guard says, "Yes?" I said, "I'm with the Mets." He said, "Really?" I said, "Yes." He said, "Do you have any credentials?" I said, "No, but Harvey said that I should show up." "Oh Harvey told you that, huh? Harvey who? Who's Harvey?" I said, "Well, Harvey, the clubhouse guy." "Well, Harvey didn't tell me. Did Harvey leave any kind of authorization with you?" I said, "Oh man, well, why don't you call Harvey?" "I don't know Harvey's number. Do you know Harvey's number?" He was totally busting me. It's clear he's not letting me in.

Finally, as I began to pull my cell phone out to call Harvey, the Met team bus arrived. The guard said, "Oh, if you're with the Mets, the Mets are gonna know that you're with the Mets, right? Here they are."

AL LEITER was the first major league pitcher to beat 30-different Major League teams. Leiter retired during spring training in 2006.

Remember after the first game I had been sitting with Al Leiter and John Franco, so I'm standing there, and the guard's standing right next to me. The bus door opened, the first guy who got off the bus was John Franco, and he just like waved to us, "Hey Bruce…" And I just walked right in. That was neat.

I was in heaven. The Mets lost both games, but this was back in 2000, the year they went to the World Series.…

The first baseball game I ever went to the Mets beat the Dodgers 1-0 with Tug McGraw on the mound. Sandy Koufax was pitching for the Dodgers. That would have been 1965 or 1966. The guy's record was like 25-1 against the Mets in his career—something incredible. Tug McGraw was the starting pitcher that day. He went on to become known as a relief pitcher, but he beat Koufax 1-0.…

The year the Mets won the Series in 1969, Campbell's Soup did a promotion. Before the game, about fifty kids were divided into three groups. Tom Seaver talked to us about pitching, Cleon Jones talked about hitting, and Bud Harrelson talked about fielding. My father was in the supermarket business and he had a videotape which I've transferred onto a VHS, no sound. You can see me and my little brother and Tom Seaver is showing us how to hold the ball.

At one point, you can see Seaver is asking something like, "Does anyone want to try this?" The next thing you see is my hand going up, and next, you see Tom Seaver in his uniform squatting down like a catcher and Bruce Laxer, 11 years old, firing in the ball. I look at the videotape once every couple of years.…

THEY MAJORED IN MINORS

Dick Fox

Dick Fox is retired in Celebration, Florida, and spends his summer on Cape Cod. He was in the product-sampling business with companies called Campus Pac in Mt. Vernon, New York, and Superbox.

My wife and I got married in early '65 and moved to New York City. We started going to all the Mets games. It was never very crowded out at Shea Stadium, but it was a wonderful summer because as soon as the ballgame was done, we'd just walk over to the World's Fair. It was absolutely wonderful. But, many weekends that summer, as well as the following summer, we would go to Williamsport, Pennsylvania, where the Mets had an AA team. The reason we went to Williamsport is that my college classmate and teammate, Shaun Fitzmaurice, was playing there. He had signed a big bonus with the Mets; yet he only played 13 games in the big leagues with them.

One day at the swimming pool at the Holiday Inn in **WILLIAMSPORT**, we're sitting across from Whitey Herzog, who was the Mets Director of Player Personnel. What was amazing about Whitey is all the players loved Whitey—even the guys that weren't playing. He knew what he was doing, and he was honest with the players. Everybody knew that Whitey was the key to the Mets winning the championship in '69. He later got fired from the Mets because he got so upset that the

> **At the Little League World Series in WILLIAMSPORT— for $16 total—a family of four can each get a ticket, program, hot dog and soda.**

Mets gave away Amos Otis to Kansas City. Anyway, one day at Williamsport, the day we met Whitey, Whitey said to me, "Hey, do you want to go scouting with me this afternoon?" I said, "Where are you going?" He said, "I'm going to Philadelphia to look at a left-handed pitcher. As you know, the Mets have the first choice in the draft this year. I've got it narrowed down to a catcher from Hamtramck, Michigan, named Ted Simmons, and a left-handed pitcher from suburban Philadelphia, named Jon Matlack." I told him I was there to go to the Williamsport Mets game tonight. He said, "We'll be back for that." So, Whitey Herzog and I went on a scouting trip to see Jon Matlack. He pitched a great game that day, and may have been the reason the Mets took him with the first overall pick in the draft that year....

Another guy we befriended at Williamsport was Hank McGraw, who also had been a big Mets bonus-baby from California. Ironically, he had a younger brother who was spending that entire summer with the Mets on the major league roster, although he hardly ever got in a game. That was, of course, Tug McGraw. Hank McGraw was great.

The next year was when Tug got sent down to Jacksonville; Fitzmaurice was playing there along with several of the other guys who later made the Mets. Most of them lived in the same apartment complex. I remember Ken Boswell and Kevin Collins shared an apartment. They were trying to "wallpaper" the apartment by stacking empty beer cans to the ceiling. Tug was seeing this young lady named Betty, who was from Louisiana. I can't remember if she was a hairdresser or a dancer—I think she was a hairdresser. Of course, little did we know, until years later, that they had a union that summer that produced Tim McGraw. But, of course, none of us knew that at the time...and neither did Tug.

The Mets also had a player in the minors named Greg Goosen, a catcher from California and a great looking prospect. At a young age, he made the Mets for a cup of coffee. Casey Stengel, one time, said, "Greg Goosen is 20 years old. In 10 years, he has an outside chance of being 30."

One player we befriended in Williamsport and Jacksonville was Kevin Collins, a great guy from Springfield, Massachusetts. He also had spent the entire '65 season on the big club, along with Tug McGraw. I remember one day at Shea Stadium when Kevin Collins got three doubles off of **JUAN MARICHAL** and almost had a fourth one. He only had a handful of doubles in his entire major league career.

Another time, at spring training, the movie, *The Graduate,* had come out in early 1967. There was a scene in the movie where Benjamin Braddock is banging on a church window screaming, "Elaine. Elaine," as his old girlfriend was getting married. We're at a Sweden House Smorgasbord in St. Petersburg, Florida, and all of a sudden, this guy starts banging on the window screaming, "Elaine. Elaine." It was Tug McGraw. Tug, of course, always had the million dollar smile and was always really great.

Probably the nicest couple on that team at that time was Ruth and Nolan Ryan. They were just really nice then—and they never changed over the years.

It was just so much fun in the late sixties going to Shea Stadium. They'd always have Banner Day. One of the guys who played in the minors that we would see quite often in Jacksonville or Williamsport but who never made it to the big leagues was Wilbur Huckle. The Mets fans were so knowledgeable about the Mets system that one day at Banner Day, there was a banner that said, "Our Defenses Will Never Buckle As Long As We Have Wilbur Huckle."…

JUAN MARICHAL was the winningest pitcher in the 1960s, winning 27 more games than Bob Gibson. Marichal won 25 games in a season three different years with a career ERA of 2.89. He never won a Cy Young Award.

We went to St. Petersburg for spring training. We'd always get to the Al Lang Field early and sit right behind home plate for batting practice. There'd be few fans there that early. One winter, January of '67, the Mets made a very controversial trade when they picked up an outfielder named Don Bosch from the Pittsburgh Pirates. Bosch ended up playing several years with the Mets. One day, I was sitting next to John Murphy—just in regular seats in the stadium. John Murphy was the general manager of the Mets. He knew my face but didn't know my name. He leaned over and said, "Hey, who did we give up to get Bosch from the Pirates?" Here was a very controversial trade of maybe sixty days before, and Murphy, the general manager of the Mets, couldn't remember who we traded to get him.

Another day, early in batting practice, this guy comes and sits down next to me. He's a real nerdy looking guy—just an absolute nerd. He was a car dealer from Milwaukee. I asked him what he was doing down in St. Pete. He said, "I'm talking to teams here. I'm a Ford dealer in Milwaukee. The Braves have moved to Atlanta so we're going to try to get another major league baseball team." I remember sitting there thinking, "If that guy gets a major league baseball team in Milwaukee, I'm only 20 sit-ups from getting Ann-Margret into a hot tub." He was the least likely guy ever to do that. It was Bud Selig. He got his team when the Seattle Pilots folded after their first season in 1970....

I feel sorry for the young kids of today. I know I sound like an old person when I say that...but I am an old person when I say it. In our day, we would go to a ball diamond and play until dark. There were no parents there. There were no umpires. In my opinion, Little League has ruined youth baseball, because unless there's some organized practice where a kid can throw the ball only 20 times and swing the bat 10 times, nobody goes to the baseball diamond.

When we were young, we remembered the day we first saw television. Then, we remember very well the day we got it in our
house, and how we'd stay up until ten o'clock at night and start
watching the test patterns. Or, we'd get up real early in the
morning and watch the test patterns. Even though our parents
didn't fall in love with our music, they, at least, listened to it.
There were not many major arguments over the music scene.
You could understand the harmless words. When we would date
a girl, we would treat her with respect and with manners...and
she didn't dress like a slut. Once a year, maybe, we got to take
the railroad train car several hundred miles to go to a major city.
We had baseball cards—not as an investment but as fun. Our
kids will never know the joy of any of those things.

It's almost a turnoff going to major league games today and
watching how fundamentally horrible most of these major league
players are. Very few outfielders can throw accurately to any
bases anymore—there may be three guys in the big leagues that
can: Vladimir Guerrero, Jose Guillen, and Ichiro Suzuki. After
that, hardly any outfielders have strong or accurate arms. Catchers, on a play at the plate, will try to catch a ball in foul territory,
which allows the ball to hit the runner, plus it takes longer to
reach the catcher. Today, in the major leagues, there may not be
one outstanding manager. Most of the managers are strictly
cookie- cutter type guys. The pitch count is just ruining the
game. Because of the pitch count, pitchers are not allowed to
develop strong arms. As long as you don't let young kids throw
curve balls, they can throw fast balls forever and never hurt their
arm. Perhaps the primary reason that the U.S.A. lost the World
Baseball Classic was most of the other countries had better fun-
damentals and played with far more passion....

In 1968, during spring training, even though the Mets had
spring training in St. Petersburg, they were opening up the
season in San Francisco. They had exhibition games in Phoenix
and then Palm Springs on their way to San Francisco. We went

to the games in Phoenix and then we went over to the games in Palm Springs. The beer vendors were the same guys in both parks. Three of us were in Palm Springs one night, and we go to a hot place called the Howard Manor. We're sitting in the Howard Manor and, I have no idea why we decided to do this, but we told our waitress and other people around us that we were Mets players and were in town for the exhibition games the next couple of days. I was Tom Seaver. One of my buddies was Ken Boswell. The other buddy was Ron Swoboda. The guy who was playing Ron Swoboda knew nothing about baseball at all. We're going along, laughing and joking with this whole group of people. They're treating us with all this new-found admiration and asking us for autographs. I looked up. There was Jerry Koosman coming through the front door. Fortunately, he sat down at the bar. I knew Koosman a little bit, but not very well. I went over to him and said, "Hey, Jerry, here's what we're doing over there. Can you play along with us?" He said, "Yeah, that'll be fun." We invited him to come over and sit with us. Once Koosman was sitting there, it just leant more credence to who we said we were and what we were doing. We were eating and drinking free all night long. The owner of the Howard Manor, a guy named Lou somebody, came over and introduced himself, and he bought us more drinks. Then, he invited us back to his house in Palm Springs afterwards and literally had a party for us…a great party.

The next day, I go out to the ballgame, but the other two guys don't. My friend who played Kenny Boswell is in downtown Palm Springs at a department store, paying for something with a credit card, when Lou's wife walked up to him and said, "Hey, Kenny, why aren't you out at the ballpark?" He said, "I was, but I pulled a hamstring during warm-ups so I showered early." He dodged that bullet. Then, the very same day, the new ***SPORTS ILLUSTRATED*** came out, and there was Ron Swoboda on the cover. Anyway, we had just a fun time. We got a glimpse, for a day or so, what being a New York Met player was like.

One time, we went to Philadelphia to watch the Mets play a series with the Phillies. There were six of us. While crossing that big bridge going into Philly, the guy driving the station wagon said, "Boy, I wish I had my console TV with me." Most TVs in those days were either these big consoles or little portable jobbies. We looked at him and said, "Console TV? Why would you want your console TV with you? They won't let you take a TV of any kind into the ballgame." The driver said, "Yeah, I know that. I know that. But, if I had the console TV with me, we'd have our tickets, 'cause right now they're sitting on top of my TV back in Scarsdale."

The best selling issue in the 50+ years of ***SPORTS ILLUSTRATED*** is the 1989 Swimsuit Issue featuring Kathy Ireland on the cover. *Sports Illustrated* subscribers have the option of bypassing the Swimsuit Issue and having their subscription extended one issue...less than 1% exercise that option.

IT WAS A FOOLPROOF PLAN AND THESE WERE THE FOOLS THAT PROVED IT

Stephen Alepa

Park Ridge, New Jersey native Stephen Alepa, 39, will never forget Game 6 in the 1986 World Series—the abuse Mets fans took from Red Sox fans, and the taste of sweet victory when Mookie Wilson's ball went through Buckner's legs. Alepa lives in Andover, Massachusetts, where he's a software executive.

During Game 6 of the 1986 World Series, there was some black-tie event at **GEORGETOWN UNIVERSITY**. We diehard Mets fans were too young to appreciate 1969, and we had been waiting for this moment all our lives. The band leader made an announcement that the Mets had lost the World Series. "Congratulations to the Red Sox," he said. Fights broke out between Mets and Red Sox fans, everyone thinking that the Mets had lost the World Series, only to find out, about half an hour later, that the World Series was not over. The Mets had miraculously won Game 6, and there would be a Game 7.

Fast forward to Game 7—Mets win! We were celebrating—all these Georgetown guys who were Mets fans and had just found each other at Georgetown. Maybe there was some genetic feature that attracted us to each other. We were dumping beer on each other's heads as if we were in the Mets locker room. Then this one guy, Phil Fahey, who always came up with silly ideas

> **Paul Tagliabue once held the career rebounding record at GEORGETOWN. That mark was broken by Patrick Ewing in 1985.**

said, "Let's go to the parade." He just threw the idea out there, and everyone kind of pooh-poohed it. Everyone said, "Yeah, yeah, right." Here we were, at two o'clock in the morning, with beer poured over our heads, all drunk. "How are we going to get to a parade at eight o'clock tomorrow morning in New York?" I said, "Hey guys, I think we can do it. Here's what you need to do. Go home. Get a change of clothes. I'll be by to pick you up in twenty minutes." "What are you doing?' they wanted to know. "Don't worry about it. Just go home. I'll pick you up," I said.

As part of my work-study program, I drove the Georgetown athletic teams back and forth to the airport, so I had the keys to the van. I used to drive Patrick Ewing around. I thought, "What's the harm of me borrowing this van for a few hours in the middle of the night?" So I got the van, which was one of those long stretch vans with three or four bench-row seats. I drove around and picked up each of the guys. They all said, "I can't believe we're doing this."

On the drive from Washington, we continued the party—drinking, smoking, celebrating. People started to drop off asleep one by one because by now it was four in the morning. I remember someone waking up somewhere on the New Jersey Turnpike, trying to figure out where the heck he was, and saying, "Holy cow, we did it. We stole a van, and we're going to the parade."

We made good time. We drove to my parent's house because we didn't know what else to do with the van. My mother was in the driveway, just leaving for work, and she said, "Hey guys, what are you doing here?" She asked us, "Can I make you breakfast?" So, she made breakfast for us.

We told her we had borrowed the van and were going to the parade. We all looked and smelled like we had been drinking and partying for the last fourteen hours...because we had. But my mother, being the saint that she is, got out of her car, went right back inside and made scrambled eggs for everybody. She was probably forty-five minutes late for work that day.

The parade was great. We were life-long Mets fans just soaking up the victory. We got back in the van later that day and drove straight back down to Georgetown because I didn't want the van to be gone too long, thinking someone was going to be looking for a stolen van. When we were about three or four blocks away from campus, some of my friends began to get uncomfortable and started asking, "Hey, why don't you let me off here?" They didn't want to be with me when I drove through the gates at Georgetown. They thought they might be arrested. It was no big deal for me, but the fact that everyone else was nervous started to get me nervous. There was one guy left in the van when we pulled onto campus. I parked it right back into the spot I had taken it from fifteen hours before, and slunk away like Bill Murray in *CADDYSHACK* after he blows up the gophers.

The next day, the Georgetown **SOCCER** team was driving the van up to a game somewhere in Maryland when they were in an accident. Now, the captain of the soccer team was one of the guys who had partied after the game and would have come with us to the parade if he hadn't had a soccer game. He was in the van and may even have been driving. The cops were investigating the accident and noticed beer cans and cigarette butts rolling out from under the seat. The cops were saying, "Wait a

> The Professional **CADDIES** Association (PCA) has 2,800 members and is headquartered in Palm Coast, Florida. Until 2002, the PCA's Hall of Fame was located in founder Dennis Cone's Winnebago.

> More U.S. kids today play **SOCCER** than any other organized sport, including youth baseball. Perhaps, the reason so many kids play soccer is so they don't have to watch it.

second. Are you sure you're going to a soccer game? Tell the truth here." My friend, the soccer team captain, knew the whole story, but he never said anything, and the cops just chalked it up as an accident, which it was....

When I was about 10 years old, I made up a game that I would play every day by myself. I would take a tennis ball and throw it on the side of the house and, basically, play a full nine-inning game, the Mets versus whoever they were actually going to play that day. If it happened to be a doubleheader against the also god-awful San Diego Padres, I would play that doubleheader out. I knew the lineups that would be batting for both teams, who would be pitching, and so on. I'd throw the ball against the chimney, and I'd be the fielder. How the ball came off the chimney would determine what kind of hit it was. If I threw the ball really hard, it would hit off the top of the chimney and go over a fence behind me, and that was a home run. If I just threw it against the chimney, it would be a single, double, or triple. I'd play double plays, things along those lines. I'd play the game out, and pretty much every game would end up the same way. The Mets would be losing going into the bottom of the ninth, or into the ninth inning. Dave Kingman and/or Lee Mazzilli—who were the only two bright spots—if you can call them that, on that team at the time, would invariably step up, somehow, in the ninth inning and hit a home run to win the game.

Occasionally I'd add a little drama in my mind, and we'd go into extra innings. We'd go to the twelfth or thirteenth inning and Kingman or Mazzilli would come up again and hit another home run to win the game. I did that pretty much for every Met game in the summertime. Maybe, I might have had them lose once or twice.

One time, throwing against the house, I almost killed my grandfather. Because the chimney was on the side of the house, if I missed the chimney, I hit the house. And if I hit the house in the right spot, objects hanging on the wall inside the house would fall off. And if I hit the *right* shingle on the outside of the house just perfectly, the ball would knock down a metal lamp that was hanging on the wall. I did that once. The lamp hit my 75-year-old grandfather in the head and drew blood, but he was fine....

My parents were always amazed that I would watch every Mets game on TV even when they were awful. It would be a beautiful, sunny summer day, and even if the Mets were playing a **DOUBLEHEADER** against the Padres, the two worst teams in baseball, I would spend eight hours in front of the TV. And that would be after I had already simulated the game against the house. Thinking back, those are some of my warmest childhood memories.

> **In 1944, the Chicago White Sox played 43 double-headers. Last year, they played one....In March, 1954, the Lakers and the Hawks played a regulation, regular season NBA game using baskets that were 12' high rather than the usual 10'...the next night they played each other in a DOUBLEHEADER. True facts, believe it or not!**

the formula for the magic number is actually a recipe for chili

A LOT OF OLD PEOPLE LIVE IN FLORIDA...WITH THEIR PARENTS!

Craig Nardi

Craig Nardi, 44, lives in Florida but still maintains his Mets Satur-
day ticket plan. Because he grew up in a Yankees family, he feels that
the family reunions should be held at Dysfunction Junction.

During the week of the 1973 World Series, I complained about being sick because back then there were a lot of day games, and I didn't want to miss any of them. Even the games out in Oakland started at four o'clock, and I wouldn't get home from school until four o'clock. I missed school a couple of days and my mother said, "You're not sick." She got wise to the idea of me putting a match to the thermometer and stuff. I really did do that.

After a couple of days of just missing school totally, she sent me to school. I went to the nurse after lunch and said, "It must have been something I ate. I'm sick. I have to go home." They called my parents, and my mother said, "Oh, he has to stay in school. We don't believe it." I convinced the nurse that I was sick and was able to go home. My mother was really mad at me, but at the age of eleven or twelve, it didn't mater. I wasn't yet interested in girls so the Mets were the big love of my life at that point. They were in the World Series against the Oakland A's— Rollie Fingers, Gene Tenace, Reggie Jackson. To me that was more important than my mother grounding me for a week....

When Seaver was traded, I was pretty much heartbroken. I didn't think Pat Zachry and everybody else was really going to be able to take his place. I was just devastated. I attended school in Providence, Rhode Island at Johnson & Wales University, a cooking school. It was about a five-hour drive to Shea Stadium, but I would still go. The games would be over at 10:30-11:00 at night, and my roommate and I would drive back to Providence, get home at 3:30 or 4:00 in the morning. We would have to go to class at 7:00 a.m.. We would be so exhausted that we would stop for coffee and arrive to class late. I would be able to go to class late four or five times each of two seasons, and use various excuses, before the professors got wise. Then, the next year, new teacher, same thing.

One morning, one of the instructors saw our cups of coffee and said, "I want to talk to you guys after class." He asked us why we were always late on particular days, and I said, "Well, we were in New York last night." "Why did you go to New York?" I said, "Mets game." He said, "What's more important, your education or a baseball game?" I said, "You really don't want me to answer that." He said, "Well, it's not going to happen anymore because I'm not going to allow you in the class if you're late anymore."

Well, I didn't stop going to the games, and true to his word, he locked the doors once class started. A couple of times we would go to class and have our cups of coffee in hand. We'd try to get in the classroom and the door would be locked. He'd look at us through the glass and wave to us, "Good-bye." We would go back home and back to bed. Fortunately, we both were able to miss particular days and still get passing grades. My friend was a Red Sox Fan—most of my friends are Red Sox fans and we got along pretty well until 1986—but I convinced him to go with me by reminding him he'd get a free game ticket, free ride to the game, and free parking. So, he'd go with me and root for the Mets.

I moved to Tampa, Florida, a few years ago, but I still renewed my Saturday plan ticket, which means every Mets Saturday home game, I have tickets. So, every Saturday when the Mets have a home game, I fly from Tampa up to New York, go to the

Saturday game, stay overnight, and then return the following day. I may miss a couple of the early-season games, but out of those thirteen games I have, I can realistically see myself attending ten of them, not including playoffs. I've had Mets tickets for many, many years, and during baseball season I'd drive on a weekly basis from Glastonbury, Connecticut, to Shea Stadium, about three hours each way door-to-door.

When I'm at Shea Stadium, sitting in those stands and the sun is shining, the green grass is on the field below you, then the team comes running out on the field—whenever that happens, I still get that same feeling inside me that I did when I was a 12-year-old and went to my first game. It's almost like a little kid walking into the living room on Christmas and seeing all the presents under the tree. It's that kind of high.

Flush twice.
It's a long way
to Yankee Stadium.

WRIGLEY FIELD—
THE LAST REFUGE OF SCOUNDRELS

Frank Ciatto

In the summer of 1988, 22-year-old Frank Ciatto left his Jersey City home with his buddies and toured major league stadiums.

We tried to maximize how many different stadiums we could get to. We actually missed Anaheim, Texas, and Seattle—Anaheim and Texas because the home teams just weren't there when we were, and Seattle because this was pre-Ken Griffey, Jr., and the team was terrible. The drive to the Kingdome was about a day and a half out of the way, so we made a conscious decision not to go.

We tried to see as many Met games as we could along the way. We were in Wrigley Field. We had a lot of friends in Chicago, so we were going to stay for one, maybe two, games. We wound up staying for three games—on Thursday, Friday, and Saturday—of a four-game set against the Cubs that year.

By the Saturday game, we were all feeling incredibly comfortable in Wrigley, where the fans are great. As much as I love Shea, sentimentally, I've always said that **WRIGLEY FIELD** is the best place to watch a baseball game. So we were there very early before the Saturday contest. We were trying to get players' autographs and balls thrown to us, that kind of thing.

> **In 1994, the White Sox recalled Michael Jordan from Double-A Birmingham to play against the Cubs in the Mayor's Trophy Game at <u>WRIGLEY FIELD</u>. Jordan singled and doubled against the Cubs.**

There was a classic exchange between our friend, Alex, and Roger McDowell. Alex, a die-hard Mets fan, was hoping to get a ball and was screaming from the left-field bleachers at Roger McDowell, who was shagging flies. "Roger, Roger..."

Alex is screaming at Roger McDowell, and Roger McDowell is his usual fun-loving self, just soft talking with someone, ignoring everyone, but especially ignoring Alex, because Alex is screaming at the top of his lungs. Finally, it must have been—and I may be exaggerating, but I don't think so—fifteen minutes of constantly barraging Roger McDowell, calling "Roger, Roger"—because Roger was catching fly balls and throwing them into the stands to fans—and nothing. Roger McDowell was throwing them to girls in tanktops and anybody else but a 5'8" screaming maniac.

After fifteen minutes, Alex yells to Roger, "That's it. You are off my Christmas card list," at the top of his lungs. So, of course, Roger McDowell, with the sense of humor that he has, turns around and says, "I didn't get last year's card." Alex was totally taken by surprise. He stumbled his way through. "I sent it. I sent it," he yelled, and sure enough, Roger McDowell threw a ball to him. There were many non-Met great moments on that trip, but that one was probably the pinnacle for us Met fans....

When I think about the guys who had a way of changing the fate of the franchise, I can name four that definitely jump out at me: Tom Seaver, Dwight Gooden, Keith Hernandez, and Mike Piazza. Piazza is in that demigod class right now. When I was a kid, though, I loved Tug McGraw. As a lefty, I always had a real affinity for left-handed athletes. In those days, they didn't make replica jerseys the way they do now, but I had this wool thing that my mother bought. I went for Halloween as Tug McGraw four straight years. Tug McGraw, Lenny Dykstra, both those guys were traded to the Phillies—they were bad trades. But you could write another book on the bad trades they've made over the years.

EXTRA INNINGS

Now comes the 2000 NLCS, and my wife and I have to go to London. Game 1 was on Wednesday and I saw that. Then Thursday night, the next night, was when we left New York for London. I knew I would never get American sports coverage, except for maybe the Super Bowl, in a European paper. So every day, I had ESPN fax me the two or three-page game story to the Comfort Inn in Kensington. The guy behind the desk wondered what these people from the States were faxing. He thought we were really crazy. But I needed to know. A chance to go to the World Series—I was hanging on every play. I knew the Yankees were going to be in the World Series because they're the Yankees. But the Mets had a chance—this could be it—what everybody in New York had been waiting for since 1956.

Just before we left to fly back to New York on Tuesday, I had received the fax that the Mets had won the fifth game and were one game away from the World Series. But, in fact, because of the time difference, the last game had already been played, and since we had checked out, I didn't know whether they had made it to the Series or not.

I sat on that seven-hour, American Airlines flight just dying. "Did they make it? Did we win? Are they going to the World Series?" We got off the plane and my wife went to the baggage claim area. I saw a man holding up a newspaper at eye-level, with the front and back pages facing directly out, as though he were holding a billboard. There it was in big letters: METS WIN, or METS ARE IN, something like that. I thought, "Oh my God, they're going to the World Series. I don't believe it." The Yankees had not yet clinched the American League championship, so the Subway Series wasn't set, though in my mind, the Mets would be playing the Yankees because the Yankees were the Yankees. It never occurred to me that the Yankees wouldn't go.

——**BARRY ABRAMS**, 34, Bristol, CT

In 1963, my girlfriend Nancy and I made a trip down to Louisiana to visit her parents for the first time. As we drove through Arkansas, we came upon a grocery store that Elwin (Preacher) Roe, the old Brooklyn Dodger pitcher, was operating. It was a country-type grocery store with a porch out front in the middle of a relatively rural area. As I paid for my Coke, I asked The Preach—I guess as a joke, because he hadn't pitched since 1954—whether he might consider a comeback with the Mets, who were pretty much brand new. Roe said, "Naw, that Casey Stengel is too mean!"

My wife, Nancy, and I were married on June 21, 1964, which happens to be the day **JIM BUNNING**, who was with the Philadelphia Phillies at the time and is now a U.S. Senator from Kentucky, pitched a perfect game against the Mets. It kind of cast a pall on my honeymoon, and was, I'm sure, an omen portending the eventual collapse of the marriage. At the reception, a friend told me about the perfect game. I was really upset, but I certainly had to take it in stride considering the other activities of the day. I did have occasion to see Bunning in recent years because I'm a journalist and have covered the U.S. Congress, first for Reuters and then for the U. S. Information Agency. I kind of harassed Bunning about it, and told him that he had wrecked my marriage. Bunning was unrepentant. He just smiled it off.

In the early years, the Mets were so inept, and maybe I relate to ineptitude. When Reagan was president, I covered an automobile dealers' convention that he addressed. A guy was walking through the hotel wearing a big name tag that read, "Hobie." How many Hobie's can there be? I asked him if he was Hobie Landrith, and he was. He was amazed that anybody would recognize him or remember him from that 1962 Mets team.

———RALPH DANNHEISSER, 66, Journalist

> When current Kentucky U.S. Senator **JIM BUNNING** retired in 1971, only Walter Johnson had more career strikeouts than Bunning.

Several years in a row during the late 1980s, my friend Sheila and I went on an annual Mets road trip. In 1987, we went to Wrigley Field in Chicago and had the worst time at any ballpark ever. Some of the fans there were drunk and unruly. We went to mid-week day games, two days in a row, and were sitting in the reserved grandstand—not even in the bleachers. We had been warned not to wear Mets garb or we would have a problem, so we purposely didn't wear anything that had a team logo or colors on it. We also were warned not to stand up and applaud or yell for the Mets.

We were very quiet, and the first day, we were sitting in the reserved grandstand when a couple of guys came along. They were already tanked. They kept calling the beer vendor over for more beer and became drunker and drunker. They realized after an inning or two, we weren't cheering when everyone else was cheering, so this guy immediately behind me leaned over and screamed in my ear, "Mets suck! They play in Queens, bunch of faggots!" I thought, "I can't argue with a drunk. There's no point to it." I never said anything. I just leaned forward so he couldn't yell directly in my ear.

He got involved with his friends again so I leaned back in my chair. But then he started to pat the top of my head. Again, I never turned around—I never said anything to him. I just leaned forward so he couldn't touch me. After a little while, I sat back again. Then, he kicked me in the back. I could tell that it was no accident. I didn't do anything to him, but I turned to Sheila and said, "Okay, I've had enough. This is too much for me. I'm going to get a security guy."

I stood up to leave the row, and he stood up and dumped his beer on top of my head. I had still not said a word one to this guy. I was livid, as you might imagine. I found a security guard, and told him what happened. He told me, "We have a police station here in the ballpark with a holding cell. We can arrest him, but you're going to have to give a deposition at some point and you might have to come back to Chicago from New York and testify....Or we can throw him out." I said, "You know what. Keep him in the holding cell for a little while, and then throw him out."

Even though they didn't arrest him, I had to go down to the little police station at the ballpark to make out a report. I missed about three innings, and I smelled like a brewery.

The next day, Sheila and I came back for the second game. We were sitting one section over from where we had been the day before, and a different group of drunk guys sat down. After a couple of innings, they realized that we were Mets fans and they started throwing hot dogs with mustard at us. I turned to Sheila, and said, "All right, this is too much for me again." I stood up and one of the guys dumped his beer on me for the second day in a row. So, once again, I went to find a security guard, and of course it was the same guy. He said, "Weren't you here yesterday?" I said, "Yeah." He said, "What's up with you?" I said, "I'm sitting here with my friend, two women, we're not saying anything to anybody, and this is what we get." They had to throw a different group of drunk guys out for a second day in a row. I don't recommend Wrigley Field for Mets fans.

——**DEBBIE ROSENBERG**, N.Y. comedy writer

I remember once in Philly, we tried to get to the stadium. One night, we couldn't get in so we asked some people where could we see the game telecast? They were laughing and sent us into this bar. The game was about ready to start. It was one of those times when Rose was going to break the record. So, we were hurrying to get in this bar. We run in there, go right in the bar, and it's one of these transvestite bars. I now knew why that guy was laughing. We ran in, and there were all these transvestites, and we were looking for the ballgame, and there was none of that over there. We went out to the parking lot by the stadium. Sometimes, it's just good to hang out there. You hear things, and you talk to people. That's baseball.

——**FRANK CIVITELLO**, Brooklyn

Yankee fans' ego applied for statehood today. If approved, it would be the third largest.

Chapter 6

Metsapaloosa

THE WORLD WAS DIFFERENT WHEN HE STARTED WORKING FOR THE METS—FOR ONE THING, IT WAS FLAT!

Bob Mandt

No person has been with the Mets organization longer than Bob Mandt. He started in 1962 at the **POLO GROUNDS** *and, for many years, was the Mets ticket manager. Shea was to be completed in 1963, but when Mandt moved into his new Shea offices the day before opening day in 1964, work-ers were still laying the sod and painting the fences.*

W
e had the "Mad Doctor" who was really early on in the Mets' history. His name was Dr. Principato, a radiolo-gist. He was a very nice man. They called him 'the Mad Doctor' because he would wear a raincoat and would exhort the crowd. He would be in loge section 4, which was a pretty good section. He'd buy sixteen tickets for each of certain games. He would pack those seats with pals of his. He was a good earner. He was no jerk. He was a smart guy. He had a flourishing prac-tice. His hands had to be operated on, and he wound up going down to Florida. I totally lost track of him. I don't know if he's alive or dead.

> **The tower lights from the POLO GROUNDS now illuminate Phoenix Municipal Stadium, the spring training home of the Oakland A's...the A's wear green and gold colors because of former owner, Charles O. Finley's fondness for The University of Notre Dame.... The Green Bay Packers' colors are also green and gold because Curly Lambeau played at Notre Dame and loved ND's color scheme.**

There was a lady by the name of Joan O'Connell who used to come with her husband. It was a pretty funny thing because, to get the best seats she could get, she took two seats back-to-back, and we used to call those "mother-in-law" seats—when you had one seat behind another. She would put her husband behind her, and she would sit in front of him. Eventually, she asked if she could get an extra seat, and we were able to shoehorn another chair in there so she wound up buying three seats.

There was a guy by the name of Egmont Lazko, a retired man, who always came with a pair of brown sneakers. He would bring his lunch, a very clean type of guy, but wore thread-bare clothes. He was retired, and his love and passion was the New York Mets. He was a foreigner from Eastern Europe. He would come to every game year after year after year. He had a great seat, too, because sometimes you have a single that you can't get rid of, so he had a really good seat.

Pearl Bailey latched onto Hodges and the '69 Mets, as did Mayor John Lindsay. The Mets probably got Lindsay re-elected because it was the year of the terrible snowstorm, '68-'69. All of Lindsay's efforts were directed at Manhattan, and it was the snowstorm where Queens was the "forgotten borough." That was the quote that was used in all the newspapers. The streets were impassible. Not only did we not get any plows going up and down side streets, but the Whitestone Expressway, which was a major road that goes from the Whitestone Bridge, was never plowed. Cars were abandoned on that particular parkway. That Parkway connects the Grand Central Parkway with the Cross Island Parkway, a major road, and also takes you to the Whitestone and Throg's Neck Bridge. There are other ways to get there, but you have to go through side streets and a lot of the side streets were impassible. So he was castigated tremendously by Queens residents. It happened to be the year that he was running for re-election. Lo and behold, the Mets made a run for it.

As we got closer, Lindsay became ubiquitous. He was at Shea all the time. There are plenty of pictures of him in our locker room when we won the pennant and World Series. Of course, the election was the beginning of November—we had won the World Series in October—so I would say we had a great deal to do with him being re-elected, the fact that he had made that identification with the Mets. He was a nice man, by the way. He was a very liberal Republican who eventually ran as a Democrat.

New York had a lot of problems at that point, both racial and economic, so his reign is not remembered all that fondly. He was an interesting character. He was a patrician-type guy, an Ivy-League type person, and elegant. He did a lot to diffuse a bad racial situation. He had personal integrity and courage—there's no doubt about that—because he did go out and quell a lot of would-be riots. He was brave.

There are a number of individuals who are season tickets holders now who have had them since the Mets started. Al Rappaport was one. I saw him not too long ago. I sold him the box up in the Polo Grounds, so we're not talking Shea Stadium, we're talking two years in the Polo Grounds.

There's a guy by the name of Cal Liepper who is in the rug business. He bought his seats off of a fellow who is a buddy of his who had the seats originally up in the Polo Grounds. His name was Freddie Kaufman who was in the meat business. Freddie and Cal were good friends. When Freddie retired, he sold his seats to Cal, but Cal had been part of his retinue for quite a while anyway. When I sold the seats to Freddie, he was a pretty rough guy, and he was very, very nice. He came from Brooklyn. He called me up at the Polo Grounds and wanted to buy eight seats. Well, eight seats was a phenomenal sale. You were getting twos and fours, and here's a guy who wants to buy eight seats. I said, "Well, can I make an appointment with you to come up to the Polo Grounds and take a look at the seats?" He said, "I have no time to be going up there. I'll take your word for it. Where are these seats?" I said, "Well, I happen to have a very nice eight-seater on the third base side, not the Mets side, but the visitors third base side. They are above the aisle. You won't have any problem with anybody walking in front of you. They are about the eighth row of boxes between third and home." I said, "I really wish you'd come up and look at these, though." He said, "Hey, look, if the seats aren't any good, I know where to find you." We became very, very good friends. He was a really nice guy. Later on he sold his seats to Cal, who still comes. I see Cal all the time. He's behind the dugout.

When Mrs. Payson was the majority owner of the club, other owners were Luke Lockwood, and a guy by the name of G. Herbert Walker. There was no 'Bush' attached to it. He was George Bush, Sr.'s uncle and brother of Prescott Bush who was a senator from Connecticut. M. Donald Grant was one of the owners. Jim Carlisle was another one. As Casey Stengel would say, "All of these people are currently dead."

When you went up to the Polo Grounds to meet someone, to show them their seats, it was a trip. First of all, the Polo Grounds had been virtually closed since the Giants left in 1957. The only events that went on up there were some stock car races. So, in 1957 the Giants left, and in 1960, the Titans started—now the Jets. The Titans drew flies so a lot of seats had been cannibalized. If they were missing a seat in the infield, they took a seat from the outfield. The place hadn't been painted in years. It was a dump. We tried to play at **YANKEE STADIUM**. We were turned down by the Yankees. Under general manager George

> **Thomas Edison sold the concrete to the YANKEES that was used to build Yankee Stadium. Edison owned the huge Portland Cement Company....Edison's middle name was Alva, named after the father of one-time Cleveland Indians owner, Alva Bradley.**

Weiss, the Mets thought the only way we're going to draw and make any kind of an impact was to have some "name" players, even though they might have been over the hill. But Houston, which was virgin territory, was able to take young ball players like Rusty Staub and develop them. That's really why during the first several years, Houston used to kick our pants. We had big names but they couldn't play anymore.... The Polo Grounds hadn't been used in years, and now we can't play at Yankee Stadium so we had to paint the place, refurbish, it and fix it up. It cost about a million bucks—the number I always heard, and it's probably fairly accurate. A million dollars in those days was a million dollars, not like today where it would probably be twenty million dollars. We were down at the Hotel Martinique on Thirty-second Street which was a real dump. Howard Clothes, who was an early sponsor, had given us a basement down there—probably rent-free. We had our ticket office down there, and there were executive offices on Fifth Avenue. After the Polo Grounds was painted and cleaned, we moved up there in March of 1962. We'd take the D train up to Harlem because the Polo Grounds was on Eighth Avenue and One Fifty-fifth Street. It was a broad street—Eighth Avenue is a broad block, and the wind in the wintertime would come whipping down. You'd be standing on the street corner freezing, dreaming of spring training.

Prospects for season tickets would go out into this desolate ball park with the wind blowing and the prospect would always say, "Are you sure the Metropolitans are going to be ready to play baseball?" We'd say, "Yeah, sure..." not knowing whether we were or not. Normally I'd get back on the D train and ride back down to Thirty-second Street where our office was. One day, a fan named Al Rappaport was there. He was very short, but his features reminded me of John F. Kennedy. I apologized to him. I said to him, "Can I drop you off by cab somewhere?" I didn't have any authorization to do that, but I figured the guy was buying the seats, I should treat him. He said, "No, I'll take you." He had a limo. I thought that was nuts. Here was the guy, I made the appointment with him. I'm selling him the seats, and he's giving me a ride back to midtown in a limo. It was a lot of fun in those days. We really got by with a much, much smaller staff than exists today. It was a different type of game. Guys like Ron Swoboda were so cooperative and would do things for you for practically no money. There was no money. Nobody was making big bucks like they do today. Eddie Kranepool will tell you today—he still does work for the Mets—that the dates that we had set up for him in the wintertime because he lived in New York—just going out and speaking at different Lions Clubs and places like that—got him through the winter up until the next baseball season. They would pay him thirty-five—fifty dollars an appearance. He might go out five or six times a week. Now, you can't get these guys for 20 times that amount.

Drove by the Matsui Museum of Progress today. It's still not open.

YADA YADA YADA

THE OLD MAN AND THE WEE...
AND MOM MAKES THREE

My dad came from Nicaragua in 1962. He was always a big baseball fan. In Nicaragua, he rooted for the Giants and the Dodgers. We came to Bayonne, New Jersey, in '62 when the Mets had just gotten started, and he adopted the team.

My dad had a friend who lived in the shadow of Shea Stadium. God knows how much my dad paid, but he had tickets for every home playoff game in 1986. At the time, I was attending college four hours from Shea. Basically, I commuted for two weeks. I would go to chemistry lab and blow out of class to go to games. It was wonderful. We would get there about three hours before each game and get sucked into the excitement and have dinner in the parking lot. It was phenomenal. Spending unbelievable quality time with my dad was great. Of course, the highlight was Game 7.

The Mets were always a reason for everybody to pick up the telephone when something happened—a big game or a big play. You'd call your friend, and his line was busy because somebody else would be calling him at the same time. It's the same with my relationship with my father. Not that we don't have other things to talk about, but for some reason, we could go a couple of days or a couple of weeks without talking, and all of a sudden, whether it's February or September, we just start talking about the Mets. Forty-five minutes later, we still haven't gotten off the subject. My dad and I talk just about every night during the season, twice a day when the team is doing well. During a dry year, you just find that you don't pick up the phone and call. When you have a great year, like several years ago, it seems like you're talking two or three times a day.

Sports Illustrated

MAY 6 1968 40 CENTS

THE MOVIN' METS

SLUGGER RON SWOBODA

Credit: SHEEDY & LONG/SPORTS ILLUSTRATED. May 6, 1968.

Credit: *JAMES DRAKE/SPORTS ILLUSTRATED.* December 22, 1969.

Credit: WALTER IOOSS JR./SPORTS ILLUSTRATED. April 13, 1970.

Sports Illustrated

SEPTEMBER 7, 1970   60 CENTS

PENNANT
PRESSURE

NEW YORK'S
BUD HARRELSON

Credit: WALTER IOOSS JR./SPORTS ILLUSTRATED. September 7, 1970.

The cover of Sports Illustrated reads:

Sports Illustrated

JUNE 21, 1971   60 CENTS

STRUGGLE
AT THE TOP

New York's hustling Jerry Grote

Credit: TONY TRIOLO/SPORTS ILLUSTRATED. June 21, 1971.

Credit: NEIL LEIFER/SPORTS ILLUSTRATED. May 22, 1972.

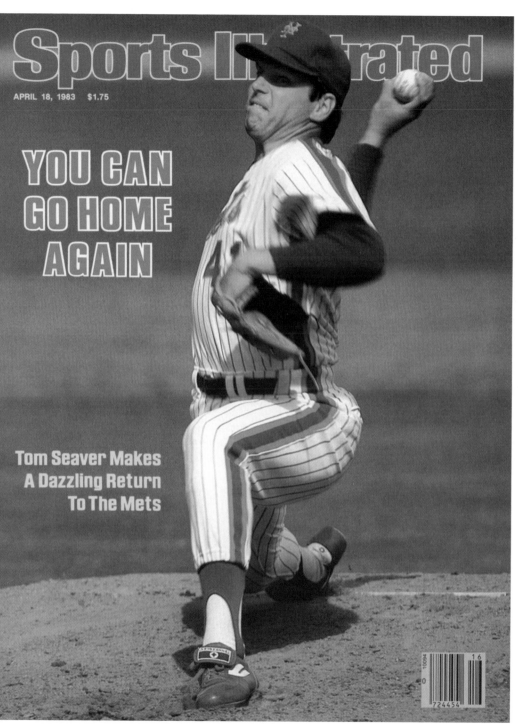

Sports Illustrated

APRIL 18, 1983 $1.75

YOU CAN GO HOME AGAIN

Tom Seaver Makes A Dazzling Return To The Mets

Credit: JOHN IACONO/SPORTS ILLUSTRATED. April 18, 1983.

Credit: HEINZ KLUETMEIER/SPORTS ILLUSTRATED. April 23, 1984.

Sports Illustrated

AUGUST 25, 1986 $2.25

ARMED FORCE

Ron Darling Of The Pitching-Rich Mets

Credit: MANNY MILLAN/SPORTS ILLUSTRATED. August 25, 1986.

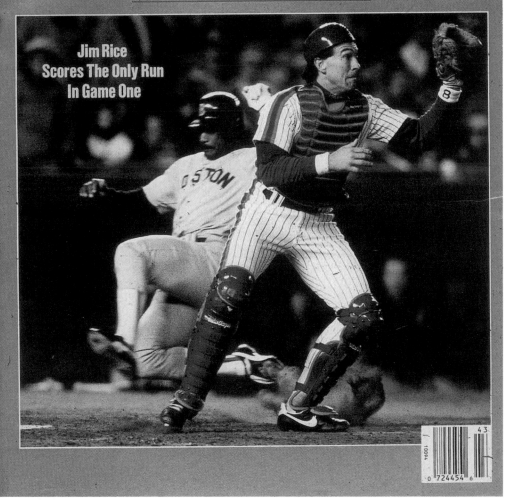

Jim Rice
Scores The Only Run
In Game One

Credit: RONALD C. MODRA/SPORTS ILLUSTRATED. October 27, 1986.

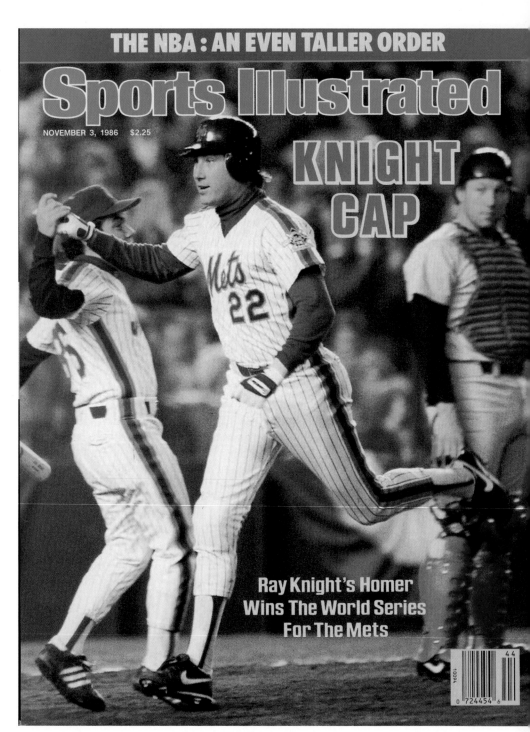

THE NBA : AN EVEN TALLER ORDER

Sports Illustrated

NOVEMBER 3, 1986 $2.25

KNIGHT CAP

Ray Knight's Homer Wins The World Series For The Mets

Credit: RONALD C. MODRA/SPORTS ILLUSTRATED. November 3, 1986.

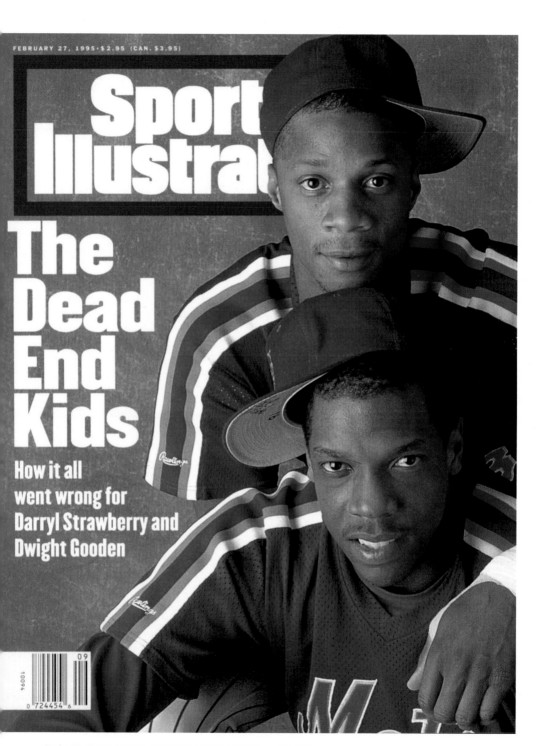

FEBRUARY 27, 1995 · $2.95 (CAN. $3.95)

Sports Illustra[ted]

The Dead End Kids

How it all went wrong for Darryl Strawberry and Dwight Gooden

Credit: *WALTER IOOSS JR./SPORTS ILLUSTRATED.* February 27, 1995.

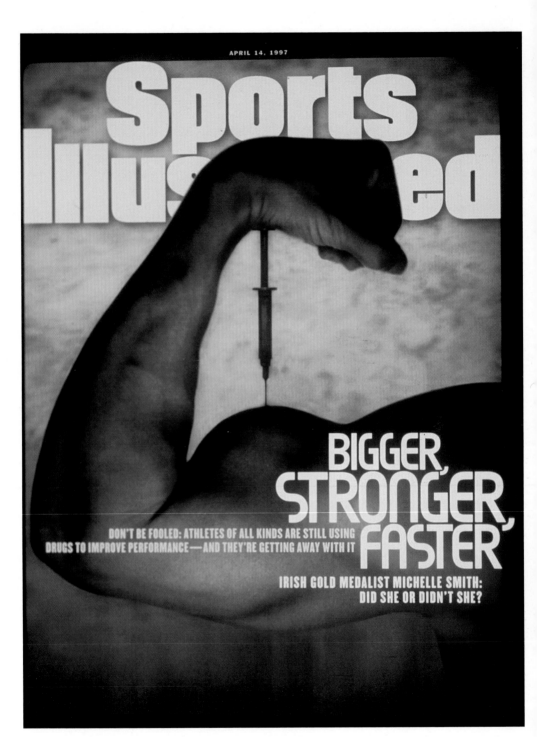

Credit: *MATT MAHURIN/SPORTS ILLUSTRATED.* April 14, 1997.

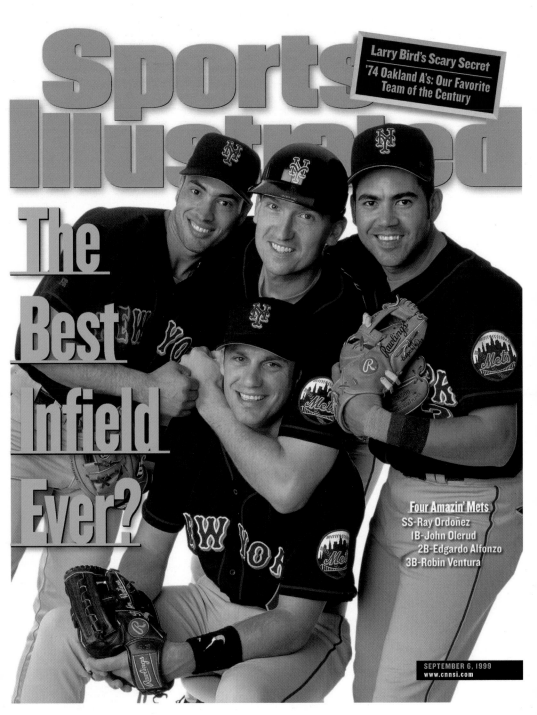

Credit: VJ LOVERO/SPORTS ILLUSTRATED. September 6, 1999.

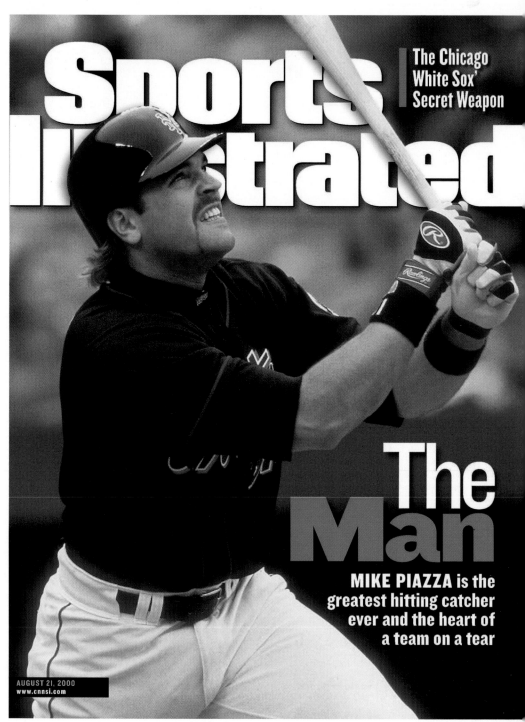

The Chicago
White Sox'
Secret Weapon

Sports Illustrated

The
Man

MIKE PIAZZA is the
greatest hitting catcher
ever and the heart of
a team on a tear

AUGUST 21, 2000
www.cnnsi.com

Credit: JOHN IACONO/SPORTS ILLUSTRATED. August 21, 2000.

My dad is a combination of Ricky Ricardo and Bill Cosby. He has a Spanish accent and sometimes mixes up his idioms. He said, "Joseph, we have clean them." I said, "You mean sweep them?" He said, "Yeah, yeah, sweep them, clean them, whatever you mean." That became the inside joke about cleaning them— "we must clean them tonight" we would say, instead of sweeping them.

——**DR. JOE GOMEZ**, 38, Bayonne, New Jersey

I will never forgive my father—not ever—for making me miss the second half of a game Tom Seaver started. My father, who doesn't like baseball very much, used to take me to maybe one or two games a year. For a guy who didn't like baseball, one year he bought tickets to a doubleheader. It was obviously torture to this man, so why would he get tickets to a doubleheader? I don't know, but he did.

I just loved Tom Seaver, and he was starting the second game of the doubleheader against Cincinnati. It was one of those terribly rainy days where the rain comes and goes and comes and goes, all day long. There were delays throughout, and the second game was delayed by forty-five minutes. It was dragging on and on, and became an entire day of baseball, and ugly. But even when I was a kid I couldn't stand leaving a ball game early. When we would go to games, my dad was always one of these people who had to beat the traffic, always had to leave—we never saw the end of the game. We had to leave in the eighth inning. He'd tell me I could listen to the game on the radio on the way home in the car. That particular day, Seaver started the second game, it was a lousy day, and it was getting late. The next day was a Monday, a school day, and I think he just wanted to get us home. I had to leave in the fifth inning. I was so upset. To this day—to this day—I'm angry with my father because he did that to me.

——**STEVE CUNETTA**, 35, Attorney, Seattle

My father was from a family of ten kids, all of whom were die-hard Brooklyn Dodger fans. When the Dodgers left New York, the National League left New York, and until the Mets came on the scene, he wanted nothing to do with baseball because he hated the Dodgers for leaving. We lived in Flatbush, Brooklyn. When I was 10 years old, I remember my uncle telling me that there was a new team to be called "The Metropolitans" in the works for the National League in New York. When the Mets were born in 1962, all my uncles and my dad became Mets fans.

In 1988, when the Mets played the Dodgers in the playoffs, my dad was sick with **LOU GEHRIG'S DISEASE** and was dying. This was to be his ultimate match-up, his ultimate revenge, that the Mets were gonna beat the Dodgers in the play-offs. I wore an old Brooklyn Dodger flannel "away" shirt that said "Brooklyn" on it and put on my Mets jacket and hat. In the bar, the Brooklyn Dodger, which is now the Salty Dog in Bay Ridge, Randall Pinkston, the New York television reporter, saw me and asked, "Who are you rooting for?" I said, "Come on. You mustn't be from Brooklyn. I'm a die-hard Mets fan, and the reason we have to beat the Dodgers is because we'll never for-give them for leaving Brooklyn." Of course, the Mets lost, and that was my most crushing blow. A couple of days later, my father passed away, knowing we didn't beat the Dodgers.

——TOMMY FLYNN, 54, Brooklyn

My first memory of the Mets comes from when I was about five or six years old. Sunday afternoons in my house smelled like roast beef because we always had a big family meal. After church and before the meal, about one o'clock, the television was always turned on to the Mets. Our family didn't have much money so we couldn't go to the games. We only had one televi-sion, and since dad always watched the Mets, you either didn't

> **Jacob Javits, Charles Mingus, David Niven and Catfish Hunter have all died of ALS—LOU GEHRIG'S DISEASE.**

participate and went to another room and read, or you watched the game with him. I had just gotten eyeglasses and was very self-conscious. I always found refuge with my dad, and I would sit on his lap and watch Mets games with him on Sundays.

Looking back, it makes for nice memories. Being a Mets fan was a birthright.

———**KATHLEEN FILAK**, 41, Jersey City

One day in 1966, my father was watching a Mets game on TV. I was six years old and didn't know anything about baseball. The Mets theme song came on, and I thought it was a television show, the Mets Show. I had no concept of professional sports. There was a big introduction by the three announcers, Ralph Kiner, Bob Murphy, and Lindsey Nelson. Then the game started, and I had to go to bed.

The next morning I asked my father, "What did the Mets win?" He said, "What, are you kidding me? They lost eight to nothing." I didn't understand. I thought I had seen the Mets Show. I thought it was some kind of roller derby where the home team won all the time. That's how I became a baseball fan.

———**JIM BAKER**, 45

My dad has these "jokes." When Mike Piazza would come up, he's not going to hit a home run every time at bat. He's just a human being. Maybe he'll strike out or ground into a double play with a couple of men on. My dad will say, "Ninety-one million dollars, and that's what we get." I say, "Dad, what do you expect?" He says, "I expect him to hit a home run every at bat if he's going to get ninety-one million dollars."…

———**JOHN ZIPAY**, 39, Houston

I watched Game 6 of the 1986 World Series with my dad. I was so utterly shocked seeing the ball roll through Bill Buckner's legs that it was the only time in my life that I can think of that I had no idea how to react. I literally sat glued on the couch and babbled, "Haaaaah." I didn't realize how important to me the moment was until ten years later when the Mets were still going through their crappy period. For my twenty-fourth birthday, my dad bought a picture of the ball taken from down the first base line just after it went through Buckner's legs. It was signed by Bill Buckner and Mookie Wilson, who had hit the ball. I don't know why, but for some reason I just broke into tears. It was just like the Mets had been so bad for so long and that had been a special moment I had shared with my dad. He didn't expect me to react the way I did. That picture brought back a lot of memories.

——MARC BECK, 33, Queens

WhAts the difference between Dwight Gooden ANd government bonds?

Government bonds mAture.

HOT DATES, COOL MATES

I had a relationship that paralleled the Mets 1990 season. This gal and I started dating in June, right after I had graduated from high school. As the Mets were going along and doing okay, so were we. Then later in the season, the Mets absolutely caught fire. Darryl Strawberry picked that team up and carried them on his back, getting big hit after big hit. I remember taking this girl to a game and seeing Strawberry hit a game-winning home run, and our relationship kicked into high gear after that. We were getting along like gangbusters. Then, I went away to college, I went through that period where I was obsessed with the Mets and they were beginning to sputter. The long distance began taking a toll on our relationship. About the time the Mets were dropping that doubleheader to Montreal, I think she was about ready to throw a drink in my face. It's an interesting parallel. Baseball and relationships. There's a fine line. A fine line indeed.

———PETER FORNATALE, 33, Long Island, NY

Every year, I make humorous Christmas cards. A lady I dated was named Robin, and I was going to try to get a picture of her with Mike Piazza and write the caption, "Happy Holidays from Batman and Robin." But first of all, I couldn't figure out how to get Piazza for it, and then, by the time it got close to Christmas, she and I were no longer an item.

———RALPH DANNHEISSER, 66, Manhattan, Baltimore

One of the biggest stumbling blocks early in my relationship with the woman who became my wife, now my ex-wife, was that I wouldn't be able to watch Mets games on television if I moved from New York to Seattle, where she lived. We dated long distance, and then she said, "If you move to Seattle, I'll buy a satellite dish so you can catch the games." That sealed the deal. I moved to Seattle and eventually married her, but she reneged. That might not have been a direct reason or have anything to do with the fact that we're no longer married after ten years, but doesn't it say a bunch?

——**STEVE CUNETTA**, 46, Seattle

In high school, I dated a guy who was probably even more of a Mets fan than I was. It was almost to the point where I wanted him to choose between me and the Mets. He had the Mets on television every night. If the game went eighteen innings, it didn't matter, we saw it through to completion. Any chance we had to go to a Mets game, we went. I actually have a picture of this guy and myself standing next to cutouts of Dwight Gooden, which we paid for. I was in my twenties. We never really did anything that didn't involve the Mets. It's not like we would go to a Mets game and then to a Broadway play. It was just the Mets. And eventually, it would be he and I and my brothers going together to Mets games.

We were at a doubleheader once, and it was a nasty day. The Mets were playing the Astros. It wasn't an exciting time. The Mets weren't in the playoff hunt or anything like that, and I didn't want to be there. The first game had gone into extra innings. I was so bored; I looked out and said to him, "I can't believe that **FENCE** is 358 feet tall."

He looked at me and shook his head and said, "Don't even tell me." I said, "What?" He said, "What are you talking about… 358 feet tall? Darryl Strawberry's not even 7 feet tall. Look behind him." He went into tirade, and I realized then what I said, and I thought it was pretty funny. He got so angry. He yelled, "How could you say that?" I said, "Take it easy, it's no big deal." I was a very good student, but my family knows I sometimes say things before I really think them through.…I remember one game when the whole family was watching the Mets. Dave Kingman hit a game-tying or game-winning home run. The whole family was

> **During the Seattle Mariners' first year in 1977, they measured the distance to the FENCES in fathoms. A fathom is six feet. For instance, where a park may have a sign that denotes 360 feet, the Kingdome would have the number 60.…**

jumping up and down and high-fiving in the living room. Then things settled down. I looked back at the TV and they were showing the replay. I go, "Oh my God, he hit another one."

——KATHLEEN FILAK, 41, Jersey City

One night in 1987, a girlfriend and I went to see a game at Shea. Her family had box seats so we went often. This was the night after Doc Gooden checked himself into the Smithers Clinic for cocaine. The guy in front of us was doing lines of cocaine, and I was this close to just tapping him on the shoulder and saying, "How about that Gooden, huh? That's outrageous. The nerve of him!"

Gooden's drug problems were in the air that night at Shea. There was a buzz in the crowd over what was happening to him. And here was this guy doing cocaine right in front of me. According to books written since then, the entire team back then was in some kind of altered state most of the time.

——JIM BAKER, 45, New Jersey

I've never understood Yankee fans in general. To me, rooting for the Yankees always seemed very much like rooting for the sun to rise. While I wouldn't say that I wouldn't date someone who is a Yankee fan, there's something better about the character of a woman who is a Mets fan, or a fan of another major league baseball club that would make her more attractive to me. As a stereotype, the Yankee fan would have a sense of entitlement. She'd be someone who is very used to getting her way. Especially if she began following the Yankees in the last five years, she'd be someone who would absolutely have no sense of how to deal with adversity. In general, she'd have an arrogance that might be less appealing to me than say a typical female Mets fan that might be more used to the world as it is. She'd be someone who understands the philosophy of "You Gotta Believe" and what that means. The great thing about being a Mets fan is not that they don't ever win. It's that they win just enough. There's something special about that.

——PETER FORNATALE, 33, Long Island, NY

'69—
THE YEAR THE METS TURNED NEW YORK UPSIDE DOWN

It's just a shame that young people under the age of 45, or whatever, will never know the experience of what the 1969 season was truly like! It was truly a miracle, truly a miracle. The Cubs were such a much better team it wasn't even funny.

Most baseball fans consider the rivalry between the St. Louis Cardinals and the Chicago Cubs as one of the greatest in baseball, but the fact of the matter is, with Cub fans, their biggest rival—the team that they hate the most after the White Sox—is the New York Mets. Most Cub fans remember the summer of '69. They remember how excited they were. Whereas, basically, for most baseball fans living today, the Cardinals and the Cubs have never been really good at the same time. So, you talk to a Cub fan, the number one team they hate is the Chicago White Sox. The number two team they hate is the New York Mets. And then, the Cardinals come in as their third most-disliked team.

In one three-week period of time, in the middle of the '69 summer, the astronauts landed on the moon, Ted Kennedy drove his car into Chappaquiddick, The Woodstock Music Festival was held in Bethel, New York, the My Lai massacre occurred, the Charlie Manson murders happened…and the Mets were surging towards first place.

——**DICK FOX**, New Rochelle resident in '69

Back in 1969, Cleon Jones appeared at a bank in our town to sign autographs. My mother took me and a bunch of friends. We all got his autograph, and my mom made the comment, "He looks like he's gonna hit a home run tonight."

Sure enough, Cleon comes up late in the game against Ted Abernathy of the Cubs and hits a home run. Being only nine years old, I was just floored that my mother could tell he was going to hit one.

Most people remember that game and remember the Jimmy Qualls' hit to break up Seaver's perfect game, but I'll always remember Cleon's home run. Now, when I visit New Jersey and drive to my parents' gravesite, I always pass where the bank used to be and remember that day.

——JIM SPOOR, New Jersey

The first baseball game I ever went to was a Mets game on September 24, 1969. I was seven years old. It was Fan Appreciation Day, but more important, in Mets lore, that was the night they clinched the National League East division for the first time. Since it was my first game, I didn't really know what was going on. I went with my parents and aunt and uncle, fully expecting to see a ball game. I vividly remember the action that night. Donn Clendenon hit a three-run homer. Joe Torre hit into a double play. Gary Gentry was the pitcher. The game ended 6-0, but the surprise for me—again, not understanding what was happening at the time—was how loud the game was. I knew something special was happening. Then, when the game ended on a double play, I watched all the fans dive onto the field. I thought, "Wait a minute here. Does this happen all the time?"

From that night on, it was love at first sight for the Mets.

——MICHAEL CASSANO, 45, Bronx, NY

I'm always amazed that I never hear anyone talk about the grass. In 1969, I went to the game where they clinched their National League pennant against the Cardinals. Clendenon hit a three-run homer in the first inning, and then they went on to win. Now, the Mets have all kinds of security, but then, when the game ended, the entire stadium flowed onto the field and tore up every single piece of turf. I took a huge chunk home and put it in my window box to grow, but it died a couple of months later.

After the playoffs, the fans ran out and pulled up the turf again. After the World Series, they did it again. I remember being out around second base pulling up a huge chunk of grass along with everyone else. There was a frenzy. The Mets had never won anything. By the time it was all over, there was no grass anywhere. Then I think the Mets must have decided to put a stop to that.

Incidentally, 2005 was the first year since 1966 that every National League field was natural grass. Yes, the Astrodome had real grass when it first opened in 1965.

———**BILL BERENSMANN**, Architecture Professor

I despise what happened with the Mets in 1969 because it just seems so unfair. The Mets won ten games in a row, and the Cubs lost eight straight in a row. I believe in my heart that the Cubs were the better team in 1969, and that somehow fate transpired against the Cubs, and that maybe for the Mets, there was a destiny that was programmed for the Mets that year at the expense of the Cubs. The Mets had this completely rotten team, and all of a sudden after what—seven years—they get to win everything and be the darlings of America. And America gets to revel in the glory of loving the Mets. They get to be this magical team in this magical year…but if you were a Cub fan and you listened to the first half of the year, you thought that was your magical year. You knew 1969 your magical year. Like maybe the whole '69 thing has just reaffirmed your Midwestern-ness. Like somebody's saying, "Hey guy, you're not supposed to dance, you're not supposed to revel, you're not supposed to jump up and down and get flat-out goofy, excited and silly. You've got to get rid of that Midwestern angst somehow." A couple of beers helps you do it!!

———**JACK WIERS**, Chicago native, Cubs fan,
later Orioles announcer

The summer of 1969 was so wonderful. I remember it well. Bruce Stark was a cartoonist who worked for the *New York Daily News*. He produced a series of full-page head-shot portraits of Mets players. There were over twenty of them published in the newspaper down the stretch of 1969 through the postseason. I still have every single one of them. I would cut them out of the newspaper every day. They're beautiful. If I ever have a big enough place or the wherewithal or the lunacy, I will have them all framed. I can name every member of that '69 team including people no one ever hears of anymore like Bobby Pfeil and Jack DiLauro. Only crazy Mets fans can name those people. I could tell you that Bud Harrelson's first name is Derrel and his middle name is McKinley. And that Tom Seaver's real first name is George, not Tom.

I grew up with the Mets. I felt like they were the young person's team. They didn't have the history. They weren't the Yankees. They weren't the arrogant Yankees. They were a brash, young, fun group of people. When they achieved success in 1969, we felt like it was success for us, too, as young people.

I remember Tom Seaver being interviewed in the clubhouse—champagne was flying everywhere. Mayor Lindsay was there, and he was being doused. Seaver had a line where he said—and his voice cracked as he was saying it—he was overcome, and he was screaming, "We're just a bunch of young kids who love to play this game!"

When the Mets clinched the Eastern Division on September 24, against the Cardinals, I went to my front window and hurled open the window. I had one of those big plastic horns that I had bought outside Shea Stadium. The day I bought it, I walked about fifty feet to take it into the ballpark, but the ticket takers wouldn't let me. A vendor tagged it for me, so when I came out of the game, I took the horn home. That's why I threw open my window and blasted the horn on my street to nobody in particular. I had no other place to use the damn thing.

——STEVE CUNETTA, 46

My wife, Carol, and I were at Shea Stadium when the Mets won the World Series in 1969. At that time, police security wasn't the way it is today. As soon as the last out was made, hundreds of fans ran out on the field and began tearing up the turf, picking up chunks of sod. It was wild delirium. Carol and I didn't run out on the field, but we were standing right down near the edge, near the fence, right near the field. Lo and behold, this piece of sod came flying into the stands. I grabbed it, and that was the souvenir we took home.

It was funny to have a piece of turf come flying through the air, but people were just so crazy. It was probably about a foot square. We took it to our home on Jasmine Avenue in Flushing and planted it in our front lawn. Of course, the word got around and kids would come to see it. It became like a shrine. They wanted to come with their baseball gloves and rub it on the piece of **TURF**, or they would just want to lie down on it. I tried to discourage them from trying to slide in on it because that would have been the end of my lawn. Eventually it grew, and I like to think it became a kind of outpost of Shea Stadium.

No one ever tried to take pieces of it. It was respected. We live about a mile from that house now, and as far as I know, it's still growing in the front lawn.

——JOE BROSTEK, 73

In 1969, they split the leagues up to eastern and western divisions. I remember buying one of these baseball preview magazines. Somebody had picked the Mets for third place. I was ecstatic. I went home and told mom, "Look, somebody picked the Mets to finish in third place!"

As excited as I was about the 1986 Mets, I don't get as nostalgic about them as I do for the '69 Mets. The '69 Mets were literally, to me, like falling in love for the first time.

——PATRICK HOGAN, 47

The few Yankee fans in school would tease the heck out of us, but we had our payback in 1969. The Mets were a 100-1 shot. They were the underdogs, and nobody believed in them, but we did—no matter how bad they were.

> **An announcer once asked Tug McGraw about the difference between ASTROTURF and grass. Tug replied, "I don't know. I have never smoked Astroturf."**

My brother Robert and I were with friends at Game 5 in 1969 when the Mets won. Our seats were in the upper deck on the last row. There was a feeling all through the game that we were going to win it. I remember thinking in about the seventh inning, "We gotta get down by the field level. We're gonna go on the field. We're gonna celebrate. This is gonna be our game." So, by the top of the ninth, we were down on the field level just waiting. The last fly ball was hit to Cleon Jones a couple of feet in front of the warning track, and as soon as he caught that ball, there was a sea of people pouring onto the field. It was so euphoric. There I was in the stands, and the next thing I knew I was on the field. I ran right by the infield just a little bit behind first base, scooped up the first handful of dirt with some of the foul line in it, and shoved it in my pockets. There were too many people running for the bases, people were grabbing dirt, pieces of grass, and everyone was screaming, going crazy.

We had carried off as much as we could stick in our jacket pockets and carry in our hands, and left the game with our dirt and pieces of sod and a banner, which said "World Champ Mets–1969." We tied it to the side of my father's 1960 Ford Country Squire station wagon, and drove home. Later that evening, while we were at a local bar, Moriarity's Café, we and a bunch of other fellows got the brainstorm that we should go down to Gil Hodges' house.

A little parade of cars was going around Hodges' block off Bedford Avenue. My friend, Charlie, was in the back of the station wagon throwing pieces of the grass and dirt to the people, and they were running in the street and picking it up. Then, we had to park the car because the crowd grew bigger, and finally the police came, and they blocked off Bedford Avenue. In fact, if you go there today, one block of Bedford Avenue between Avenues M and N is named "Gil Hodges Avenue."

We parked the car, took the banner with us and a piece of the grass, and marched along with everybody down to Gil's house. A big throng of people were there. A detail of police officers from the 63rd Precinct actually had to ring off the front of Gil Hodges' house, especially around his lawn. The crowd was big and friendly and began chanting, "Let's go Mets. Let's go Mets." Then, finally it broke into, "Gil, Gil, Gil," building louder and louder and louder. He and his wife, Joan, opened the front door and came out, waving and smiling to everybody. There was big cheering and screaming. He thanked everybody for coming. That's a vivid memory I have that I'll never forget.

——TOMMY FLYNN, 54

My mom and grandfather went to Game 3 of the 1969 World Series. Gary Gentry beat the Orioles, so the Mets took a 2-1 lead. It's sort of family lore how upset I was that I couldn't go to the game, but my mother secured an autographed '69 Mets baseball for me. I was only three years old, so it was put in a safe place until I got older.

Jersey City, where I grew up, doesn't have a lot of sprawling park land. I played the better part of my baseball life in a school-yard two doors from my house. Well, the sad ending to that story is that yes, when I was six or seven and my mother thought I was old enough to have it, I proceeded to take the autographed baseball to the schoolyard and throw grounders with it. The ball is in tatters somewhere, nowhere in my possession.

When my mother found out, she did what any mother would do; initially, she just screamed at me for my lack of diligence, but those moments tend to pass. Looking at it on the bright side, I guess from age six or seven until I put collecting behind me, I became an avid baseball card **MEMORABILIA** hawk the way most kids do. The experience wound up being pretty good. I went to law school with student loans. My wife has said to me on thirty to forty occasions, whenever we've sort of hit a crunch, or whenever I've complained about the student loans, "You can just

In the early 1990s there were over 8,000 sports **COLLECTIBLES** stores. Primarily because of eBay, there are now fewer than 2,000.

sell your baseball cards," which have been in my basement for years. I pull them out maybe once every five years to show someone the 1955 Jackie Robinson baseball card that I have.

People have always asked me, "Well what do you think your collection's worth?" And I don't know how much my collection's worth. Maybe, it's worth tens of thousands of dollars now. But it doesn't really matter because I'll never sell it no matter how much it's worth. Maybe that has to do with the autographed baseball debacle. You name it, all those guys who played in 1969 were on the ball: Jerry Koosman, Tom Seaver, Tommie Agee, Cleon Jones. With every name that I could throw out, the thought of it becomes more depressing. But I probably did get my eight grand of baseball playing in that schoolyard so that's fine.

——**FRANK CIATTO**, 38

I was a high school freshman in 1969, and I played hooky in order to go see the ticker tape parade. One parade began downtown and then another one proceeded uptown to Bryant Park, so I wound up running from the parade downtown, getting on the subway, and taking the subway up to Bryant Park so I could catch the second one. That was so exciting for us. It was the first time the Mets ever won anything.

——**STEVE ODELL**, 50, Yonkers

In 1969, the Mets started to play, and play well. My dad was a machinist, and he got the use of his company box in September that year. We were at a Mets-Astros game. They posted on the scoreboard that the Cubs had lost the day game, and the Mets had won the first game of a doubleheader. I said, "Look who's number one now." It was the first time in their history that the Mets were in first place. I've never seen a reaction like this. People didn't cheer—they started dancing in the aisles. It was like watching children. It was that kind of glee.

There was one incredible play after another, and they made it to the World Series. I went to a Catholic school and lived half a block from school. My teacher was such a big Mets fan that in the afternoon he put a TV in front of the classroom and turned on the game only with no sound so he could say he was teaching. Of course, everybody was watching the game. It came down to a fifth game. The Mets were about to win the World Series. I looked at the clock. We got out of school at 2:45. At 2:45 it was coming up to the top of the ninth inning. The Mets were gonna clinch the World Series.

I sprinted home as fast as I could. Everybody else stayed behind to watch the end, but I wanted to be home because my Mom was home. I got there with one out in the top of the ninth, and I got to watch the rest of the game with my mom. I can remember us literally jumping up and down and laughing and screaming. It was so much fun. That memory of being 10 or 11 years old and jumping up and down with your mother—I can see it. I can almost feel it. I remember the amazing thing about that year was Davey Johnson, who eventually would manage the Mets to a World Championship, making the last out for the Orioles in that series.

For years, I had this baggie in my dresser drawer. Somebody I knew was at the game, and he ripped a bunch of grass off the field. About six or seven years after that, my folks were going through my drawer. My father looked at the baggie of dead grass and said, "What the heck is this?" I guess they thought it was a bag of pot. They opened it up, and I said, "No. This is dirt from Tommie Agee. This is from 1969." I had it probably for nine or ten years sealed in a bag, along with the *New York Times* from when Neil Armstrong and Buzz Aldrin walked on the moon. So, they found this old yellowed newspaper and the bag of what looked like pot....

———PATRICK HOGAN, 47, Brooklyn

By 1969, the Mets were certainly an exciting team to watch, and it was a matter of getting a payoff for those years of wandering through the wilderness with them. Buoyant and vindicated! At the divisional clincher against the Braves, I took a small piece of sod from the field, which I still keep in a little box. I went to quite a few games during those two years. In fact, I sat in the

ORGANIST booth one night with Jane Jarvis. She was from Milwaukee, and I wrote a piece on her for the *Milwaukee Sentinel*. You know the old joke: "Who's the only person to have played for the Mets, the Knicks, and the Rangers? Gladys Gooding, the organist."

———**RALPH DANNHEISSER**, 66, Maryland

Years ago, I submitted to Channel 5 a couple of good Mets trivia questions to try to stump Bill Mazur. The late Mazur was the inimitable television sports reporter with the encyclopedic baseball mind. I actually got him with the first half of question one: The Mets have won two World Series, the first in 1969, the second in 1986. On both teams, in both World Series, there were the same three guys in uniform. Who were they?

Bud Harrelson played for the Mets in '69 and was a third-base coach in '86. Dave Johnson was second baseman for the Orioles, made the last out of the '69 World Series, and was the Mets manager in '86. The third player was Tom Seaver, who was in the dugout in uniform as a member of the Red Sox team.

My second question didn't make Mazur's show but is still Grade A trivia:

There is someone who played on the '69 Mets who was traded, and the player the team got in return ended up playing on the '86 Mets. Each performed the same feat in their respective World Series. Who are they?

Jerry Koosman was traded for Jesse Orosco…Orosco, a year or two later made the Mets, played with them for years. They each were the pitcher on the mound when the Mets won. They were both left-handed pitchers and they were traded for each other.

———**BOB BROWNSTONE**, San Francisco attorney

No baseball fans in the history of the game ever had a more incredible season than Mets fans had in 1969. We went to 71

In 1969, all major league parks except two, had **ORGANISTS**. By 2006, less than half had organ music.

games that season. Ironically, one of the few games we missed was a no-hitter that Pirate pitcher Bob Moose threw on a Saturday in late September.

The '69 season should not have been that much of a surprise because the previous season, the Mets lost something like thirty-eight one-run games, but a few years before that.... When you're young, you look at your lineup through rose-colored glasses. Even though you may have a lot of unproven players, and a lot of players are over the hill, you tend to look at a team and say, "Wow! We're loaded. We'll never lose with that team. We got Ron Hunt, Ken Boyer, Jack Hamilton. We could win the pennant." Then, they end up finishing in eighth place.

The unusual thing about that '69 season was that it was the first year of division play. Not only did the Mets have to win the division, they had to win a playoff to make it to the World Series.

Remember that famous weekday afternoon game against the Cubs? The Cubs young centerfielder, Don Young, was not used to playing with people in an upper deck wearing white shirts during the daytime, and lost two fly balls. After each of the misses, Ferguson Jenkins, the pitcher, and Ron Santo, the third baseman, openly showed their disgust.

A friend of mine was visiting from Elkhart, Indiana. He had a blank, white matchbook with him. On that matchbook, he wrote, "July 8, 1969." Then, he turned it over, and he wrote, "The Day the Cubs Lost the Pennant." That was just so preposterous that anybody would talk about the Mets winning the pennant in early July, but he said, "The Cubs have had it. The Cubs are bickering. The Mets are going to win this whole thing." Well...guess what? As the season went along, weird things happened. Al Weis hit two home runs at **WRIGLEY FIELD**, and he only had about four for

More NFL games have been played in the Meadowlands than any other stadium. Until 2003, WRIGLEY FIELD held the record, even though Wrigley had not hosted an NFL game since 1971.

the entire year. I remember one game where J. C. Martin, in an extra-inning game, hit a home run down the foul line in right field for the win. One day in late September, I had lunch with Cardinals' pitcher, Steve Carlton, at the Tin Lizzie Restaurant. Carlton was a very nice guy. Anyway, Carlton said, "The Mets might win the pennant, but they'll never beat me tonight." Well, the Mets beat him 6-0. Ed Charles hit two homeruns.

The night before—just to show you how lucky the Mets were that year—it was the last of the eighth inning and a tie game. The Mets had a man on first, nobody out, and Ron Swoboda was at the bat. Swoboda was an excellent bunter. Obviously, the situation called for a bunt to move the go-ahead run down to second base. Instead, Gil Hodges let Swoboda swing away, and he hit a hard one-hopper to Dal Maxville at shortstop, the best fielding shortstop in the National League that year. Instead of an easy double play, Maxville dropped the ball—two on, nobody out instead of two out, no one on…Mets win the game.

We missed the first game of the World Series because Notre Dame was playing Army at Yankee Stadium that day. The next day, we drove down to Baltimore. This was one of the best World Series games of all time. Overlooked in the Miracle Mets championship of '69 is the game that Jerry Koosman pitched that Sunday in Baltimore. It was absolutely outstanding. Then, when they returned to Shea Stadium for game three, it was just a three-day beautiful unbelievable run to the championship.

After game three, we went to Madison Square Garden for the **KNICKS** opening night… After Game 5, all the evening newscasts led off by playing the "Hallelujah Chorus." It was truly just a magical year.

——DICK FOX, 64, formerly from Scarsdale.

The first NBA Game was at Toronto's Maple Leaf Gardens in 1946. The KNICKS beat the Toronto Huskies 68-66.

I'VE KNOWN KINER AND MURPH MY WHOLE LIFE...BUT I NEVER MET THEM

My group of friends had a joke. Back in the eighties, the sponsor of the New York Mets was Schaefer Beer. Schaefer's tag line was "Schaefer, the one beer to have when you're having more than one," which is one of the all-time great tag lines. Murph would occasionally do these live spots where they actually went to a commercial break and, right in the middle of the break, they would come back to Shea and Murphy would be on camera reading a live promo for Schaefer Beer.

There was one spot—and my friends and I would do it all the time—where he would read through the copy and be ready for the tag line. They'd zoom in on Murph's face, get close to him, and he'd have the mike. He'd say, "Schaefer, the one beer to have, Mets fans, when you're having more than one...nuuuuh... hhhhh..." The screen would fade to black, but'd they leave his mike on, and you just heard him dragging the word one.

On Tankard Day, Murphy would say, "It keeps your hot drinks hot and your cold drinks cold." Who uses the word tankard? Do you even know what a tankard is? We wanted to know, "Why don't you just call it a mug?"

"Met Tankard Day. First 20,000 on a paid admission."

——KEVIN MARTINEZ, 38, Seattle Mariners

Bob Murphy was there since day one, and when it's snowing, and I'm shoveling the driveway under six, seven inches of snow, I still offhandedly come out with, "It's a beautiful day for baseball."

It wouldn't matter whether it were sunny and seventy-five degrees, or snowy and forty, Bob Murphy would always start, "It's a beautiful day for baseball."

——BARRY ABRAMS, 34, suburban New York, Connecticut

Kiner's Korner was such a wonderful postgame show. Ralph would always have a player or two from whichever team won—it wasn't always just Mets who appeared. I remember one September when the Mets were really surging. They hadn't won that particular game, though, so he had a player-guest from the opposing team. He was really very diplomatic. "Well I'd really like to wish you well, but you know how it goes," he would say.

You could tell he was a big Mets fan. His enthusiasm was totally with the Mets. Win, lose, or draw, it was Ralph Kiner. The show was so comforting. If the Mets played on the West Coast, the game would end late in New York, and my dad would say, "Time for bed." I'd always say, "Well, *Kiner's Korner.* I have to just finish up and watch *Kiner's Korner.*" His show was the official ending of the game. He would give a recap, tell who the Mets were to be playing the next day or two, what cities they were traveling to, who would be pitching. A Mets game wasn't complete unless I could watch *Kiner's Korner.* It was so folksy. There were just two chairs and a microphone, not the glitzy stuff like new on **ESPN** today.

——**ANDREA MALLIS**, Oakland, CA., Astrologer

I loved to tune in to Mets games before they started just to see the jackets Lindsey Nelson would be wearing. They were so bizarre, so hideous, but that was his trademark. I remember there was one he had that had Little Orphan Annie all over it with her dog, Sandy. I never heard a word he said because I was so fascinated with what he was wearing.

It's a running joke with long-time Met fans about how Ralph Kiner should never be on radio because he's watching a different game from the rest of us. On television, you can get away with it because you can look at the game and see that he doesn't

> The only reimbursement an athlete receives for being in an **ESPN** commercial is a one-thousand-dollar donation to his charity of choice.

know what the heck he's talking about. First of all, he's stupid, and second of all, he drinks. We're pretty sure he drinks in the booth. We can't swear to that but we're pretty sure.

Several years ago the Mets were playing a five o'clock game in Montreal. I was on the bus on my way home from work, and I put my headphones on to tune in the game. I wanted to find out what's happening. What do I hear? I hear Ralph Kiner on the radio. I just can't believe my ears. I hear him say that unfortunately Bob Murphy has had some kind of seizure and was hospitalized and so he was filling in, doing the radio play-by-play.

Ralph Kiner has a problem pronouncing names, let's start with that. He just can't get names right, and if it's a hard-to-pronounce name, that's even worse. When Gary Carter came to the Mets in 1985, for a season and a half, Kiner kept calling him Gary Cooper. And he was corrected every time. Someone would say, "That's Gary Carter." He'd say, "Oh yeah." Then of course he would have to say Carter's name the next day, and he'd say Gary Cooper again. Darryl Strawberry was on the team at the same time as Carter. Kiner kept confusing Strawberry's name with Marv Throneberry who played with the Mets in 1962 and 1963 when they were terrible. He kept calling Strawberry "Darryl Throneberry." Again, he would keep being corrected, but it went on the whole season, and it became very comical.

Then, I'll never forget when *Kiner's Korner* got Mitsubishi cars as a sponsor. He kept saying, "Wootsabushy." He kept trying to fight to say it, and just couldn't get it right. So, here he was on this radio broadcast that I was listening to on the bus ride home from work, and I'm just beside myself listening to this— giddy, knowing I was going to get some good laughs. I know something's coming. The Mets were batting and there was a hit —"Well-hit ball. Long fly ball. Going, going—caught in front of the warning track." In front of the warning track, not even at the wall! Not even a running catch on the warning track! Kiner's delivery has been a long-running joke with Met fans for years, and I just burst out laughing. The joke is if Ralph Kiner is calling a fly ball—"hit way back, way back, going, going—caught by the shortstop." That's the running joke, and I said, "Oh my God, it's real." I just burst out laughing hysterically. I know everyone on the bus was wondering what I was laughing about.

In that same game, one of the Mets hit a sharp ground ball to the shortstop of the Expos who, at the time, was Mark Grudzielanek. There's Ralph Kiner, and he says, "A sharply hit ball, hit to…," and you know he looked down to his little crib sheet that told him who's playing where, and you can just tell that he sees the name "Grudzielanek." I heard the hesitation so I knew exactly what he was doing. There's no way he's going to be able to pronounce this. No way. So I'm waiting to hear what he's going to say. He says, "A sharply hit ground ball to … the Montreal shortstop." I knew that Grudzielanek was the Expos shortstop and I said to myself, "Oh I can't wait to hear how he tries to say this," but he didn't. I almost fell out of my seat on the bus I was laughing so hard.

There was a Japanese player, a pitcher, Takashi Kashiwada, who played on the Mets in 1997. As soon as we heard that the Mets had this guy on the spring training squad, we said, "Oh, we can't wait to hear what Ralph Kiner does to this guy." When I heard Kiner announce one of the spring training games and he said the guy's name correctly, I thought, "I wonder how long he practiced that?"

I've always kicked myself that I didn't own a VCR in 1986 when *Kiner's Korner* had Yogi Berra as a guest when Yogi was a coach for the Houston Astros. It is the funniest interview I've ever seen.

They start *Kiner's Korner*, play a little music, then they show some Yogi-isms. You know like, "When you come to a fork in the road, take it." Then they show Kiner sitting there with Yogi, and Kiner says to the camera, "You know a lot of people think that the things that Yogi says don't make sense. I think they make perfect sense." It just deteriorated from there. It was hilarious. It was like the blind leading the stupid.

———**DEBBIE ROSENBERG**, N.Y.C. comedy writer

THE EVIL EMPIRE TALKS:
YOU CAN ALWAYS TELL A YANKEE FAN,
BUT YOU CAN'T TELL HIM MUCH

My parents emigrated from Greece to Brooklyn, where I was born, and they were soccer fans so the neighborhood kids turned me into a Yankee fan. When I was about five years old, we moved out of Brooklyn and into what seemed to be a "Mets neighborhood": Garden City, New York, on Long Island. At that point, being a Yankee fan marked you as being "different." From the get-go, my brothers and I took pride in being the "Yankee kids" on the block. For the longest time, until the Yankees became champion caliber again, which wasn't until the late seventies, we were always putting up with the obnoxious Mets fans who had won a championship in the interim.

——GEORGE PHILIPPEDES, 45, Long Island, Boston

Where I grew up, less than ten miles away from Shea Stadium, you were either a Yankee fan or a Mets fan. I was a Yankee fan. We had lived in Massepequa, Long Island, until I was in the fifth grade, and people there rooted for both the Yankees and the Mets, so I never felt that being a Yankee fan was a bone of contention. We moved to Garden City in 1969, which was probably the worst year for a Yankee fan to be alive, having to watch the Mets go all the way and beat the **ORIOLES** in the World Series. It was painful getting ranked on for being a Yankee fan. Also, I was new to a school system. Our first school trip was to *Newsday* newspaper, on the first day after the World Series ended. As part of the tour, we were given copies of the front

Since 1977, John Denver's "Thank God, I'm A Country Boy" has been sung at the seventh-inning stretch of every **ORIOLES** home game.

page. You can imagine what that was like for me. The front page was in color, too, and back in '69, that was a big deal.

—— **LEO EGAN**, 45, Long Island, Queens

My girlfriend, Sue, and I have been together about ten years. She was already a Yankee fan when I met her. I would never have dated a Mets fan. I once hired a guy who was very good at his job, but a month later I realized he was a Mets fan, and I always felt like he was a bad hire just because he was a Mets fan. I can't believe I went through that whole interviewing process and I never asked the most important question: "Are you a Mets fan or a Yankee fan?"

—— **DAN McCOURT**, 55, central New Jersey

The Mets weren't in existence when I started rooting for the Yankees. There was no National League team at all in New York at the time, so the Yankees became my team, although to this day I hate the Mets. Their fans are loudmouthed. You hear them complain, "Well the Yankees buy this and buy that. They just bought themselves a World Series." This is foolishness. The Mets spend just about as much money as the Yankees do. They're just jealous. I'd be jealous too, if I was in their shoes.

—— **STEVE KOHLREITER**, 55, Fort Lee & Washington Township, NJ

Mets fans just seem like superficial fans to me. There's less substance there than in Yankee fans and Red Sox fans. I think the Yankees, in a way, capture the essence of New York more than the Mets do. The Yankees and their fans, to a certain degree, are about being brash and saying, "We're gonna beat the best. We're gonna be the best. We're gonna be the richest." Be whatever. And they're not afraid to call that shot and then to go out and try to do that. Yankees are a perfect fit for New York. It doesn't surprise me that at the end of each Yankee game, especially when they win, they play that Frank Sinatra song, "New York, New York." It truly is who the Yankees are.

—— **GEORGE PHILIPPEDES**, 45, Boston Doctor

I live in Florida, where I guess it should be hard to make your sons Yankee fans. When I asked one of my kids why he became a Yankee fan, his answer was, "There was no choice." Actually, there was no choice, because their Uncle Phil tried to make my kids into Mets fans.

One day I was gone and Phil was with my kids, talking about the Mets. He had bought them Mets hats. He told my kids, "When your dad comes home, you have to tell him you love the Mets and hate the Yankees." He was doing his best to get me crazy. The kids were about nine and seven at the time, and Phil was doing everything he could to get them to say they were Mets fans.

Mets fans are always on the defensive because they have more to prove. They're always trying to attack the Yankees. Yankee fans just act like, "Hey, it's cool. It's the Yankees." I don't hate the Mets, but I find that most Met fans hate the Yankees.

So I told my kids, "You can't live in my house if you're a Mets fan. You're just going to have to move in with Uncle Phil." The kids said, "No, no, no, we don't want to do that."

——**LARRY LIEBERMAN**, 48, Palm Harbor, Florida

There's a doctor where I work at Boston Medical Center who is a big Mets fan. Recently, I'd been giving him a lot of grief about the Mets, especially when we beat them in the World Series. When the Yankees lost one of the 2001 World Series games to Arizona, every time Arizona would score a run, my beeper would go off, and the score would be featured: 1-0, 2-0, 4-0. This happened until 12:30 a.m. Finally, I called him at home and told that S.O.B. that he'd better stop it or I was gonna come get him!

——**GEORGE PHILIPPEDES**, 45, Long Island, Boston

While Yankee Stadium was being renovated in the mid-seventies, I went with a couple of friends out to Shea Stadium to watch the Yankees play. I was fifteen or sixteen years old and we took the subway. Growing up in the city, we didn't have a car so we always relied on public transportation, and it was a big deal to get to Shea. We had to take two different subway trains and it took about an hour and a half to get there. I remember thinking how strange it was going to see the Yankees at Shea. Being at Shea just felt weird.

——**PAT CANTWELL**, 46, Bronx, New York, Southern California

My hatred of the Mets stems from being in college when the Mets were really successful in the 1980s and the Yankees weren't.

I went to college at Syracuse University, where there were a lot of Mets fans. Of course, I was home in the summer, but in April and September I was back in Syracuse listening to the games on the radio. The Yankees didn't win much, so I didn't worry about October. I worked at the college radio station, and I was the only girl in sports. The guys I worked with are still my friends, but a ton of them were Mets fans.

In 1986, I had to live through a Yankee fan's worst nightmare: the Mets playing the Red Sox in the World Series. It was like being a second-class citizen in a two-team town. Your natural hatred is with the Red Sox, which you grow up with from the day you start rooting for the Yankees, but the Mets became the team to envy because they were great then, and the Yankees were terrible. It was really frustrating. The Mets always got the back page of the newspaper, and the Yankees get one teeny article in the middle of the paper. That made me a definite Mets hater.

——**LISA DUNLEAVY**, 40, Westchester, Manhattan

The Mets were so bad when they came into being in 1962 that I thought my college team could give them a run for their money. That's exactly how I looked at the Mets. But I have to give them all the credit in the world. The Mets developed that team from the ground up and little by little, year by year, they became stronger. I had a friend from high school who didn't like the Yankees, and because the Dodgers had left New York, like most Dodger fans, he became a Mets fan. Up until 1969, I belittled him about his having to leave my house at night to watch the Mets games, and then I kept quiet. Then he got on me. He would say, "The tables have turned. Now you're rooting for a loser." I said, "I can't argue with you when you're right."

——**BILL MANGER**, 59, Paterson, New Jersey, Oklahoma City

I grew up deep in the heart of Brooklyn, and it was fun to razz the Dodger fans. After the Dodgers moved to Los Angeles all the fun went out of it because there was nobody to razz anymore. I would never have razzed Mets fans. They're subhuman as far as I'm concerned. They're idiots. Well, what can I tell you? The Dodger fans you liked to razz but you didn't hate them. But the Mets fans are so conceited. They think they've got a team now, and they don't.

——**STAN STARMAN**, 74, Brooklyn, Florida

I would never have dated a Mets fan. I can barely talk to a male or female who's a Mets fan. I just can't carry on a conversation with them. Yes, I absolutely do mean that. Seriously, I cannot deal with it.

If I met someone who was nice and we were talking and the subject turned to baseball, and I found out they were a Mets fan, I would immediately harass them. My response would be, "Oh, I'm sorry to hear that, really. How can you be a Mets fan? How do you live with yourself?"

I play in a 40-and-over softball league, even with my bad knees and back. I'm following Mickey Mantle's career. I have a few Mets fans on the team that I'm really friendly with, and as a group we go to at least one Mets-Yankee game a year. It's out and out war, especially in the bar after our softball game. We go to the Beechmont Tavern in New Rochelle. It's near **IONA COLLEGE**, so you get

Thirty years ago, Bret Bearup was a Parade All-American basketball player on Long Island. At the time, Jim Valvano was the head coach at Iona. After a game, Valvano approached Bearup (who later signed with Kentucky) and introduced himself... "Hi Bret, I'm Jim Valvano, IONA COLLEGE." Bearup said, "You look awfully young to own a college."

a college crowd. Jeff Ruland of Iona College, who also played in the NBA, hangs out there, too. Our guys don't have to be drunk to get into a heavy argument or a fistfight, but I think the drinking does help.

They're all yelling so loud and continuously, they're not listening to the other guy at all. Everyone is just thinking of their team, their team, their team. And everybody around you is hysterical and laughing and drinking. They're just going at each other's throat. Basically, the Yankee fans—and I'm one of them—stick out their chests and boast their immediate superiority.

I've seen friendships end over Mets-Yankees stuff. I've had to separate guys. At the 2000 World Series, people were at each other's throats. I cannot watch a game with the Mets fans cheering the World Series. I wouldn't even want to see these people, and I'm sure they don't want to be with me either. That's the time we separate, and see each other months later during the football season. "How about that World Series?" "Don't bring up that subject."

One guy—we're actually good friends. I even give his son Mets baseball cards. He's an old Giants fan who became a Mets fan, and we're involved with Little League, and our families are really close, but the one problem is he's a Mets fan. It's horrible to say. It's his one bad point.

The Mets fans are at a distinct disadvantage, yet you hear all the time about the arrogant Yankee fan on the radio sports talk shows: "Here comes the arrogant Yankee fan." But meanwhile, how do you expect us to be? We don't care. We're proud of it. We say, "You know, you got your two pennants, 1969 and '73. You won a World Championship in '86. Come on. There's no argument here." We're laughing at them. The more it goes on, and the more laughter, the more irritated they get.

——JOE SANTOIEMMA, 53, Bronx, New Rochelle

It was easy to be a Mets fan in 1969. I knew they were the frontrunners. They didn't impress me. Then in 1986, the Mets won that dramatic NLCS against Houston…then won the World Series when Buckner let the ground ball go through his legs, it was impossible to be in New York. Everyone became a Mets fan for that period. I remember sitting in Tony Roma's restaurant during Game 6, that endless, extra-inning, Mets-Red Sox game. I spent hours in a rib joint on Sixth Avenue just watching the Mets slowly win. It was repugnant to me. Yankee fans had a terrible time trying to figure out who to root for because we hated both teams. There was no good outcome of that World Series so we essentially rooted for a blackout. We were rooting for somehow the games to be struck down and not played and for both teams to go home humiliated.

—— **VICTOR LEVIN**, 44, Los Angeles.

DAMN YANKEES

There are some teams I dislike, and there are some teams I detest. I've spoken to God. The Giants fueled my hatred for the Yanks because in my old neighborhood in Yonkers in the thirties and forties, you were either a Yankee or Giants fan, with a couple of Dodger fans sprinkled in there. I'm from a large family of nine brothers. We rooted for Willie Mays and the Giants, but the entire neighborhood was all Yankee fans. We had a lot of little fights and arguments over this, though you didn't worry about fights in those days. Nobody pulled a knife on you—you actually fought. So when the Mets came to town in 1962, I became a Met fan, and I've been ever since, through the highs and the lows. The Mets were always the underdogs. I think it's a natural instinct to want to root for the underdog. One of the reasons I became such an anti-Yank was because they were always the "top dog."

——**DAN ROSATO**, 74, Yonkers

When I was at the University of Massachusetts, there were a lot of Yankee fans. There were a lot of New York residents who went there. I didn't have Yankee fans for friends—you couldn't have friends that were Yankee fans. It's like when you were a kid, if there was a divorced kid in the neighborhood, you couldn't play with him. Well, if it's a Yankee fan, you can't be his friend. I would never have dated a Yankee fan. That would be excommunicatable. I wouldn't have to ask if a girl was a Yankee fan. Yankee fans generally reveal themselves pretty easily—that swagger, and that blind "adding up the wins and not thinking about the integrity of the game," things like that. You can always tell Yankee fans, you just can't tell them much.

——**DON SHEA**, 57, St. Petersburg, Florida

I have no problem with Yankee fans who are Yankee fans the way I'm a fan. I have a lot of friends who are Yankee fans, and I have no problem talking about the Yankees. I have a big problem with the Yankee fans who frequent Yankee Stadium, and they're throwing things at the other team and at fans who are wearing the other team's hats. To me, there are a lot of Yankee fans who are just sort of young, arrogant morons.

———BUD POLLAK, 56, retired high school
English department chairman

To me, George Steinbrenner is a highly objectionable human being. I think he's arrogant and domineering. I think he ruined baseball. He's as responsible as anybody for the commercialization of baseball, for the salaries that are on the other side of the moon.

I get most annoyed by the arrogance of the Yankees and the Yankee fans sense of entitlement; also, by their ignorance or willful blindness to how important money has been to the success of the Yankees. This goes back to before Steinbrenner, but the Yankees were millionaires in **PINSTRIPES**, and they always buy the aging star on waivers from the National League, or they sign "that" free agent. I don't know how people can imagine that baseball is just a sport and that the competition is fair. Rooting for the Yankees is like rooting for General Motors.

———ROBERT BELL, 57, Williams College English professor

In 1961, I'm six years old, going to school. You can't help it—the other kids around you are saying, "You don't know Mickey Mantle? You don't know Roger Maris? You don't know the Yankees?" There, I started to pick up on Mantle. Then, the kids would have all the cards, and you knew Mickey Mantle was the prestigious card to have in the Yankee order. I knew a little bit about baseball before that 12-year-old mark when I

> **The Yankees' PINSTRIPED uniforms were designed by owner Colonel Jacob Ruppert to make Babe Ruth look skinnier.**

learned about football…but the Yankee fans were so obnoxious, I jumped on the Mets when they started the following year.

My friend, Glenn—a huge, huge Met fan—is a bartender in Pippens Pub on 97th and 3rd in Bay Ridge. He's very knowledge-able about all sports. People come in all the time asking him questions about sports. It got to the point a couple of years ago, the owner told him, "When the Yankees are in the playoffs, I can't have you bartending. I can't have you behind the bar, Yankee fans won't come in." He'll tell you the Yankees are a third-world nation. If you come in there, as a Yankee fan, he'll make fun of you, argue with you, and destroy you verbally. He'll tell you Joe DiMaggio was way overrated 'cause he played in the era where there were no black players. He'll tell you that DiMaggio was the same as if Al Kaline was playing in New York. He feels that Yankee fans are the only abor-tions ever to live.

In the World Series against the Arizona Diamondbacks, I'm working for the phone company. I came into Pippins late one night and the place was packed. Glenn is behind the bar. In the middle of the bar, I see Glenn is really p----- and I'm laughing at him. I said, "Hey, Glenn, you must be having a great time." He's unusually short with me. Then, I noticed two guys in the bar with brand new Yankee hats on—the tag was still on them. They're yelling really crazy. I go near them, and they're yelling, "It's the Yankees. Go, Yankees." It winds up that these guys just came off the boat that day from Italy. They land, go find some friends, and they go out to celebrate. It's a great night. The New York Yankees are playing. They don't know anything. They just buy their hats and go out. As they're yelling and jumping up and down, they look at Glenn, and he says, "Hey, listen, you a------. I told you I hate the Yankees, and I hate you." Two minutes later, the Yankees hit a home run, and these guys start cheering and aren't even looking at Glenn. I'm watching the whole thing.

Glenn runs around the bar, through the crowd, grabs these two guys. They're completely bewildered 'cause they didn't even see him coming. He's dragging them through the crowd. Now they're trying to fight him, not knowing what was going on. He throws them outside. They're threatening to call the police. I go out and say, "What happened?" The foreigners said, "Well, we yell for Yankees, and he throw me out. Why? Why? Everybody yelling in there." I said, "Glenn, why did you throw those guys out?" He goes, "They're Yankee fans. They're foreigners. I hate them. I'm gonna close the bar."

———TOMMY BRUNO, Official Entertainment Director of Bay Ridge

One time in Durham, we're sitting around after a game. We had quite a few beers, and we had some Mets fans in town from New York visiting some of the players. We were at one of the player's apartment, a guy named Jim Dix. Dix' off-season job in St. Louis was as a professional pallbearer, believe it or not. One of the New York fans mentioned that the Mets were having a try-out camp in Laurinburg, North Carolina, starting at nine the next morning. Laurinburg was about an hour and a half to two hours from Durham. We all decided, "Hey, let's have fun. We'll go down there and go to the Mets tryout camp." We were all going to do it, and then after a while, and a few more beers, one of the guys said, "Hey, what if we go to the tryout camp and none of us get offered a contract, and then later one of those scouts sees us here at Durham, they might release us the next day." Needless to say, we didn't go to the Mets tryout camp in Laurinburg, North Carolina the next morning. Nor would we have been fit to anyway.

———LLOYD FLODIN, former Mets minor leaguer

It's unbelievable. There are a lot of closet Met fans. In the '80s, the Mets were *the* team. They were the tough guys, the nasty boys, the champions. The '90s come around, a little decline, Yankees come about. People forget about the Mets. But, during the 2000 Subway Series, our Mets stores were doing just as much, if not more, business as our Yankee stores. There are fans out there, and if the team is proving it's good, if the team is marketable, which it is today, they will outdo the Yankees. This is definitely a National League town. I am expecting a Subway Series again. I think the Mets are the team to beat in the National League, I really do. That's not because I'm a big Mets fan; although, I am.

I hate to say that, but the Mets are different from the Yankees. The Yankees are world-known. People come here to New York, and they expect to leave New York City with a memento, and a Yankee tee shirt will solidify that. Now, the Mets—you have to be a fan. With the Yankees, they'll have business no matter what 'cause they're the Yankees. No team, whether it's the Mets, Cubs, or anyone else, can even touch the Yankees, as far as popularity. But, a Met fan, if the Mets are winning, they will be the toast of the town, even if the Yankees are winning, as well.

——JOHN CAMILLERI, GM of Mets Clubhouse Stores

The Yankee fans are so used to winning. Now, it bothers me. They think it's automatic that they're always there. They talk about the 'Curse of the Red Sox'. I always tell them that 2000 is the curse of the Mets and the Yankees. All the pressure was on the Yankees. "All Yankee fans tell us about 26 world titles. Well, 2000 is one and we don't care anymore. The Yankees had to sell their soul, and they did for that series. They haven't won since." I just love it. Every year they don't win, I just keep saying it. It's finally starting to get to them. We made something happen that year. They *had* to win. They simply had to win—they knew it, too. If they lost out to the Mets, they couldn't open their mouths about the 26. That would have been over. They know they sold their souls that night. I was there. I know. I saw a little soul go back and forth.

——FRANK CIVITELLO, Brooklyn

Mets fans are genuine. Yankee fans forget how bad they were when they drafted Brian Taylor. They don't know half the crap they're talking about. They're functioning retards in my opinion. The Mets finished in last place a few years ago under Art

Howe. By the way, he was a f------ disaster. Why did a team that was so-called "so successful," like Oakland, be so willing to get rid of him. That year, the Mets finished in last place. They drew over 2.3 million fans. The last time the Yankees finished in last place, they barely drew a million.

My argument with Yankee fans is that George Steinbrenner, for all his patriotism, used to fly the Japanese flag when they first got Matsui. How do you fly a flag of a country that once bombed the United States and killed thousands of our soldiers? I do think Mr. Steinbrenner is a great owner though, because if you're a fan of that team, it's not from lack of effort.

——**BRENDAN GRADY**, Brooklyn, N.Y.

Two Americans were caught in Mexico attempting to smuggle drugs…one was a Mets fan and the other a Yankees fan. They were brought before the captain of the firing squad who informed them that he would grant each one a last wish providing that it was reasonable.

The ugly Yankee fan said he could die in peace if he could hear the Yankee announcer Phil Rizzuto say "Holy Cow" one more time. The captain said, "This is your lucky day. We have cable in the palace; our head of security is a moron and a Yankee fan. He tapes every game."

The captain turns to the Mets fan and asks if he has a reasonable last wish.

The big, good-lookin' Mets fan replies, "I sure do, *señor*!"

The captain says, "Well, what is it?"

The Mets fan says, "Shoot me first!"

IT'S HARD TO CHEER
WITH A BROKEN HEART

Tom English

Tom English grew up in the shadow of Shea Stadium in Jackson Heights, Queens. English was born there in 1965 and a brother Chris came along just a few years later..

I was a Mets fan as far back as I can remember. I was born in 1965 so it was 1968 when my dad took me to my first game at Shea Stadium. I loved baseball—playing it, watching it, reading literature about it. After my brother, Chris, was born, and my dad took us to games, we would walk through Corona, which is the neighborhood between Shea Stadium and Jackson Heights, and people would be sitting on the stoops of their apartment houses and calling out to ask us who had won. This was in the mid-seventies, but Corona was still like it had been in the fifties.

Chris didn't like baseball at all when we were young. We had Mets pajamas, but that wasn't his doing. I would try to talk to him about baseball, but he wasn't interested. Then, all of a sudden out of nowhere, about 1984 or '85, while I was in college, the Mets started to get good and Chris got really, really interested in baseball. He knew all the Mets. He watched every game in 1986. I suppose a lot of people became interested in the Mets in '85 or '86 because they had Dwight Gooden, Ron Darling—the team that won the World Series. Because I went to Columbia University and my family lived in the city, I was home on weekends. It was cool because, though he and I were very close just about all our lives, there were parts of our lives that I don't think we really knew. The only interest we had shared up until that point was politics, so when we began to share a love of the Mets, that was something we could talk about.

The year the Mets won the World Series in '86, I was a senior at Columbia and Chris was attending **ST. JOHN'S UNIVERSITY** in Queens. The playoffs were right around my midterm exams. I watched the sixteen-inning game against the Astros when I was supposed to be studying for a Russian literature midterm. The studying didn't happen. The midterm happened.

Before Chris went off for school the day of that sixteen-inning game, he set the VCR for four hours. Of course, the game lasted much longer, so we didn't get the whole game on tape. When the World Series began, Chris made sure he taped every game. I didn't see the entire Game 6, the Mookie Wilson game, but Chris and I talked about it many times over the years. After it turned out that the Mets didn't win two or three World Series in a row, we would sit down together and watch that game. If we had guests over, we might put it on, or just he and I would watch together. About this time, Chris really overtook me in interest in baseball, and I actually became a little jealous because I had always taken it as a point of pride that I knew baseball better than he. He took his interest and totally ran with it. He didn't paint his toes or anything crazy like that, but he became a total nut in terms of the Mets.

Our mother died during the 1987 playoffs, but Chris bought some champagne that he planned to open when the Mets won the World Series. I recently looked in the closet and the champagne is still there. It's nineteen years old. At this point, it's probably vinegar. The Mets still haven't won a World Series since '86, but maybe if they do win this year...

> **In 2006, the Carthage College <u>REDMEN</u> were mandated by the NCAA to change their nickname because it was offensive to Native Americans. Carthage changed it to the Red Men and gained NCAA approval for the "new" name.**

The Mets got lousy and at that point, I went to law school at Rutgers, in New Jersey. We'd call each other up about different trades, whatever was happening with the Mets. The ownership had bought a lot of superstars, but they really stunk. Still, for two years we had the Saturday plan, and went together to every Saturday home game.

I don't want people reading this to feel sorry for Chris, because they shouldn't. But he had been born with epilepsy, and in 1994, '95, his condition worsened, and we all agreed that it was best for him to stop working. Chris had major brain surgery in 1998. He was totally courageous. The surgery wasn't experimental, but it still took guts. That's what I want to try to get at by telling all these stories of his illness and how the Mets offered him some solace.

At this point, he essentially became a shut-in. I would always ask him to go with my friends and me to games, and prayed each time that he would, but he was afraid he would have a seizure at a game, which, in fact, he did once. I don't remember the specifics. He had decided to go to a game with friends. He was so excited because he hadn't been out in a while. When he came home, there was blood all over his face. He had a seizure at the game, fell on his head, and had to leave before the game ended. The reason I'm telling you this story is that he was so courageous, and he really did try because he loved the Mets so much. I'm saying that his being a fan was sort of an expression of his bravery and trying to live a little bit of a normal life.

I still went to a lot of games. What was really cool, in a weird way, is how when I came home from a game, I'd say, "Oh, did you see the game?" And we would talk about the game as if he had been there. Even now, I'm going to Opening Day in a couple of days, and I'll think about him. I've been thinking about him all spring training because I associate him so strongly with the Mets. Even though he was at home, if I went to a game, in a weird way because I saw it and he saw it, it was almost as though we were there together. He really looked forward to the games. He read all the newspapers. In fact, whenever the Mets were in the playoffs, he saved all the newspapers.

Chris was a very opinionated fan. I recently received a letter from a friend who wrote, "A lot of times, I would just call Chris up and say 'Valentine should be fired,' and we were off to the races." He was more of a "company" man than I am. He really gave the Mets management the benefit of the doubt in terms of trades. We argued all the time. He had far surpassed me in his knowledge of baseball, in general, and the Mets in particular. We never did have a real falling out, but we would fight pretty fiercely. I'm not that confrontational so I would always either give up or just say, "You're right." He had so-called facts, and I would just bluff my way through. It was funny. He was always more prepared. He had a very analytical mind. One of my friends once decided to read Chris entries from the *Baseball Encyclopedia*, just random stats from random years. Chris guessed who the players were about eighty percent of the time.

His final brain surgery was supposed to be no big deal. He had been in a lot of pain, and he'd always been an inspiration for me because he really wasn't dealt a whole lot of great cards in his life. On the way to visiting him after the surgery in mid-September 2001, I bought him a book, *Amazing Mets, The Miracle of 1969*, published by *The Daily New*s. I dated it 9/21/01 and in parentheses I wrote, "Five and a half games back. Chris, To my inspiration. Hang in there. Love, Tommy." The book was at his bedside when he died. I'm not sure he ever read it because two days later he fell into the coma that ultimately took his life.

He developed an infection in his brain, though his doctors still thought he'd recover. He wasn't able to talk, but I'd say, "Well, what do you think about the Mets? Do you think Valentine should be fired?" He didn't come out of the coma, but I would ask him "yes" or "no" questions, and he could clasp my fingers. Sometimes his eyes would be open. Each chapter of that *Amazing Mets* book was about a page or so, and for two or three weeks, I would read him one chapter every day. I still had hope. Friends who visited him in the hospital gave him a small Mets flag and a little tiny doll of Mr. Met which I still have. Anyone who knew Chris—the first thing that came to mind was Mets fan.

The Mets were on an incredible run the last six weeks of the season, so I would read him a story from the newspaper about how a game had gone, and I'd say, "You know, the Mets are going to be in the World Series just like you're gonna wake up." I was trying to say that there was the hope that the Mets would win the pennant, and hope that he would be OK.

Chris ultimately passed away December 31. He was thirty-four years old. I called a friend, a huge Mets fan, and he came over and we talked about Chris and how it sucked that he had died. I said, "Well, hold on a second." I took out Game 6 of the 1986 World Series that my brother had taped, and my friend and I watched the whole game together. At the very least, we knew that Chris was responsible for its existence.

It's weird how there was humor and sadness at the same time. It was my responsibility to make the funeral arrangements, and the funeral parlor always wants clothes. Usually you get the best clothes someone has, like a jacket and tie. The tradition is to have a wake. I said to my uncle, "You know, Chris wasn't a jacket and tie person. He wasn't a suit person." I found some tan pants and a tan shirt and a jeans jacket because that was the way he lived, and we wanted people to remember him that way. I didn't know of any ties he had so I was gonna get him a nice bright tie, like a "Jerry Garcia" tie. As soon as I made that decision, I passed a place in his room where he kept clothes, and I saw an old Mets tie of his that I didn't even know he had. I have no idea how old that skinny tie was, at least fifteen years old. So Chris wore his Mets tie one final time.

Everyone at the funeral service knew of Chris's love for the Mets. I ended my eulogy with, "…maybe he's in a place where there's no pain, where the clouds are beautiful…and the Mets are in the World Series every year."

Index

TO BE CONTINUED!

We hope you have enjoyed this first edition of *For Mets Fans Only.* You can be in the next Mets book if you have a neat story. You can email it to printedpage@cox.net (put "Mets Fans" in the subject line) or call the author directly at 602-738-5889.

Also, if you have similar stories about the Jets or Giants, email them to printedpage@cox.net (put the appropriate team name in the subject line). On any emails, be sure to include your phone number.

For information on ordering more copies of *For Mets Fans Only,* as well as any of the author's other best-selling books, call the author at 602-738-5889.

There were no actual Yankee fans harmed during the making of this book.